Industrial Policies in the European Community

Industrial Policies in the European Community

VICTORIA CURZON PRICE

Associate Professor of Economics
Institut Universitaire d'Etudes Européennes
University of Geneva

St. Martin's Press

for the
TRADE POLICY RESEARCH CENTRE
London

ISBN 0-312-41436-6

Library of Congress Cataloging in Publication Data

Curzon Price, Victoria.
  Industrial policies in the European Community.

  Bibliography: p.
  Includes index.
  1. Industry and state—European Economic
Community countries. 2. European Economic Community
countries—Commercial policy. I. Title.
HD3616.E833C87   1981   338.94   80-29161
ISBN 0-312-41436-6

Trade Policy Research Centre

The Trade Policy Research Centre was established in 1968 to promote independent research and public discussion of international economic policy issues. As a non-profit organisation, which is

privately sponsored, the institute has been developed to work on an international basis and serves as an entrepreneurial centre for a variety of activities, ranging from the sponsorship of research, the organisation of meetings and a publications programme which includes a quarterly journal, *The World Economy*. In general, the Centre provides a focal point for those in business, the universities and public affairs who are interested in the problems of international economic relations – whether commercial, legal, financial, monetary or diplomatic.

The Centre is managed by a Council, set out above, which represents a wide range of international experience and expertise.

Publications are presented as professionally competent studies worthy of public consideration. The interpretations and conclusions in them are those of their respective authors and should not be attributed to the Council, staff or associates of the Centre which, having general terms of reference, does not represent a consensus of opinion on any particular issue.

Enquiries about membership (individual, corporate or library) of the Centre, about subscriptions to *The World Economy* or about the Centre's publications should be addressed to the Director, Trade Policy Research Centre, 1 Gough Square, London EC4A 3DE, United Kingdom.

Contents

Trade Policy Research Centre   v

Biographical Note   ix

List of Tables   xi

Preface   xiii

Abbreviations   xv

1   What the Tokyo Round Negotiations Failed to Settle   1

2   Industrial Policy, the Market and the State   17

3   Industrial Policy in Selected Community Countries   43

4   Sectoral Problems: Steel, Shipbuilding, Chemicals and Textiles   84

5   Alternatives to Delayed Structural Adjustment in 'Workshop Europe'   119

Selected Bibliography   132

Index   137

Biographical Note

VICTORIA CURZON PRICE, a specialist in international economic relations, is Associate Professor of Economics at the Institut Universitaire d'Etudes Européennes and a member of the faculty of the Centre d'Etudes Industrielles, both at the University of Geneva. She was previously a Research Fellow at the Institut Universitaire de Hautes Etudes Internationales, in the same university, where she obtained her doctorate in 1973.

Dr Curzon Price is the author of *The Essentials of Economic Integration: Lessons of EFTA Experience* (1974), co-author with Gerard Curzon of *The Management of Trade Relations in the GATT* (1976) and co-editor, also with Gerard Curzon, of *The Multinational Enterprise in a Hostile World* (1977). Besides the first of the above titles, she has contributed in conjunction with Gerard Curzon, making a husband-and-wife team, to the studies of the Trade Policy Research Centre with three papers: *After the Kennedy Round* (1968), *Hidden Barriers to International Trade* (1970) and *Global Assault on Non-tariff Trade Barriers* (1972).

List of Tables

3.1 A Striking Loss (Work Days Lost in Labour Conflicts per 1000 Workers)   69

3.2 Stages in the Development of the European Community's Regional Policy   74

3.3 Number of Non-regional and Non-sectoral Aids to Industry in the European Community Examined by the Commission in 1978   75

3.4 Breakdown of Public Employees in the Working Population of Selected Countries in the European Community   82

4.1 Share of the European Community in Iron and Steel of its Principal Export Markets, 1973–78   86

4.2 European Community's Balance of Trade in Iron and Steel   87

4.3 Performance of the European Community's Big Steel Producers, 1977   87

4.4 Asymmetry in the European Community's Trading Relationships, 1978   93

4.5 Ratio of the European Community's Exports to Imports in Textiles compared with EFTA's Position, 1972–78   109

4.6 Ratio of Quotas to Domestic Production of Textiles in the European Community, 1977   109

4.7 Ratio of Exports to Imports in Clothing in the European Community compared with EFTA's Position, 1972–78   110

4.8 Illustrative Selection of Textile Products Subject to Quotas in the European Community   112

Preface

This contribution to the Trade Policy Research Centre's series of volumes on *World Economic Issues* owes its origin to the growing concern of people in general and managers in particular with the increasing governmental 'steering' of economies through measures which have come to be called 'industrial policies'. Every year the Centre d'Etudes Industrielles (CEI), at the University of Geneva, organises a symposium for chief executives of some sixty business associates. In 1978 the theme was 'industrial policy'. Little did I suspect when asked to write a briefing paper for it that I was about to enter one of the most fascinating and hotly debated areas of contemporary economics.

Until then I had worked a small patch in the great garden of economics known as trade policy. I had tried a line of integration issues that were coming along nicely, especially free trade areas, and later anti-trust and related matters. I had even gone into a broad field under intensive cultivation to a highly fashionable hybrid – the multinational enterprise. This particular ground was so thick with cultivators, however, that I was grateful for a break, for an excursion into industrial policy. I talked to government officials, visited the Commission of the European Community in Brussels, discussed the subject with the many managers who came and went at the CEI, sounded out my academic colleagues – and read.

The effort that went into producing the briefing paper was later renewed to produce this contribution to the *World Economic Issues* series of volumes.

It remains for me to thank the Centre d'Etudes Industrielles for giving me the opportunity to work on this subject, the Director of the CEI, Bohdan Hawrylyshyn, and my many colleagues for their helpful comments, my long-suffering husband who must have read different versions of the typescript more often than I, Anna Dawson, Arlette Mollerud, Batilda Vogel and Elizabeth Winch who typed them and, last but not least, the Director of the Trade Policy Research Centre, Hugh Corbet, no mean cultivator of ideas himself, whose role in this particular instance has been to use a sharp editorial pencil to prune my metaphors and greatly improve the final work.

Publication of this analysis has been facilitated by a grant to the Trade Policy Research Centre by the Ford Foundation, in New York, for occasional studies which is greatly appreciated by all concerned.

Finally, the usual caveat has to be entered, which is that none of the above can be held responsible for the conclusions and opinions reached in the study. That responsibility is mine alone.

Geneva   VICTORIA CURZON PRICE
January 1981

Abbreviations

AWES	Association of West European Shipbuilders
BDA	Bundesverband der Deutschen Industrie (Federal Republic of Germany)
BSC	British Steel Corporation
COMECON	Council for Mutual Economic Assistance
CGT	Confederation General du Travail (France)
CIASI	Comité interministériel pour l'aménagement des structures industrielles (France)
DGB	Deutscher Gewerkschaftbund (Federal Republic of Germany)
ECGD	Exports Credits Guarantee Department (United Kingdom)
EFTA	European Free Trade Association, whose Secretariat is located in Geneva
ENI	Ente Nationale Idrocarburi (Italy)
FDES	Fonds de Développement Economique et Social (France)
FSAI	Fonds Spécial d'Adaptation Industrielle (France)
GATT	General Agreement on Tariffs and Trade, whose Secretariat is located in Geneva
GDP	gross domestic product
GEPI	Gestiomi Epartaci Pazioni Industriali (Italy)
GNP	gross national product
IBM	International Business Machines Corporation, based in the United States of America
IDAB	Industrial Development Advisory Board (United Kingdom)
IDI	Institut pour le Développement Industriel (France)
IMF	International Monetary Fund, whose board of directors is located in Washington

IMI	Istituto Mobilaire Italiano (Italy)
IRI	Istituto Reconstructione Industriale (Italy)
ITO	International Trade Organisation, which was envisaged in the Havana Charter of 1947, but was never established
ITT	International Telephones and Telecommunications Inc., based in the United States of America
LDC	less developed country
LTA	Long Term Arrangement on International Trade in Cotton Textiles
MFA	Multi-fibre Arrangement, formally the Arrangement Regarding International Trade in Textiles
NEB	National Enterprise Board (United Kingdom)
NEHEM	Nederlandse Herstructureringsmaatschappij (Netherlands)
OECD	Organisation for Economic Cooperation and Development, whose Secretariat is located in Paris
OPEC	Organisation of Petroleum Exporting Countries, whose Secretariat is located in Vienna
SGI	Societa Generale Immobilaire (Italy)
SIDALM	Societa Industria Alimentari (Italy)
SIR	Societa Italiana Resine (Italy)
STA	Short Term Arrangement on International Trade in Cotton Textiles
TES	temporary employment subsidy (United Kingdom)
VAT	value added tax

CHAPTER ONE

What the Tokyo Round Negotiations Failed to Settle

Is international economic cooperation a fair-weather phenomenon? Are sovereign nations only prepared to entertain open and cooperative economic relationships with each other from a comfortable position of security? Do they not, at the first sight of trouble, run for shelter?

The barometer of international economic cooperation probably does, in a general sense, follow the economic cycle. Certainly periods of comparatively low growth and high unemployment (the 1890s, the 1930s and the 1970s) have all been accompanied by a partial or complete breakdown of the established international economic order – the extent of the breakdown being apparently linked to the depth and duration of the trough of the cycle.[1]

Inversely, the construction of a viable international economic order appears to need a protracted period of growth and full employment, which has occurred twice in the course of a century, once from 1860 to 1880, when free trade was organised on the basis of the 'Système des Traites', and again in the period 1945 to 1970 when virtual free trade, payments and investment developed on the basis of the Bretton Woods system, the institutions of which have been the International Monetary Fund (IMF) and the General Agreement on Tariffs and Trade (GATT).[2] The 1920s period proved too short and indecisive for an international economic order to be brought into being.

It is noteworthy, but not surprising (upon reflection), that however strong the institutional and legal edifices may be that are built during the economic upswings, they are quite unable to withstand the earth tremors of the downswings. This is because the outward and legal manifestations of the underlying international economic order grow from it quite naturally and reflect it faithfully. As long as the members of the international community see it in their interests to pursue policies that are generally compatible with those of their neighbours – and this, in practice, means open trade and monetary policies – the international economic order will reflect this attitude and conflicts, such as they are, will be relatively easy to resolve. The moment members of the family of nations see their links with other members of society as an onerous burden, impinging on their welfare, necessary links that remain will be fraught with tension and the outward and legal manifestations of the established international economic order will begin to droop.

This may seem a commonplace observation. Yet it is not unusual to come across people who believe that by multiplying international conferences, by drawing up and discussing numerous agenda of desirable objectives, even by signing international agreements of growing length, complexity and triviality, it is possible to improve or at least preserve the international economic order. This is not so. Indeed, a sure sign that the established international economic order is in distress is a notable increase in economic diplomacy and conferenceering, for those responsible for this delicate plant note its unhealthy appearance and multiply the outward signs of cooperation in the hope that this will somehow stop the rot.

Thus it was not the Système des Traites which made trade free in the 1860s and 1870s, but free trade – or the desire for it – which made the Système des Traites. It was not the Bretton Woods system which made trade, investment and payments almost free in the 1950s and 1960s, but the recognition of the desirability of virtual freedom of movement for goods and services which made the Bretton Woods system possible.

The international economic order has been going through a breakdown phase. The signs have been unmistakable:

(a) The multiplication of fruitless international conferences (no names, no packdrill).

(b) Protracted negotiations which by any normal input/output measure have been extraordinarily unproductive and disappointing (the Tokyo Round of multilateral trade negotiations, in particular, although worse cases could be cited).

(c) Growth of a parallel system based on the free and unchallenged use of unilateral policies of subsidisation and various other non-tariff measures, selective bilateral agreements to limit trade and exceptional sectoral arrangements of a discriminatory nature (as, for example, in textiles).

No amount of international commercial diplomacy can halt this trend as long as the majority of Western governments continue to react to the problem of 'over-capacity' in a defensive and inward-looking manner. Indeed, this visible deterioration in the established international economic order took place since 1973, during which period governments devoted much genuine effort to improving the international trading system and to liberalising trade.

Example: Subsidies and Countervailing Measures

The subsidy issue is a good example. In 1974, the United States imposed a countervailing import duty on Michelin tyres exported from Canada on the grounds that a new Michelin tyre plant in Nova Scotia was heavily subsidised, as indeed it was, but no more than many others around the world. Part of the American objection, it is true, was that from the outset it was intended that 80 per cent of the plant's output would be exported to the United States.

Canada protested vigorously and several West European countries began to worry about whether the United States might not 'countervail' some of their exports as well because producers had received a development grant of one kind or another. The United States raised the issue in the Organisation for Economic Cooperation and Development (OECD), where a Committee for International Investment and Multinational Enterprises was set up in January 1975. After eighteen months of difficult negotiations the members of the OECD produced the now familiar Guidelines for Multinational Enterprises and a rightly more obscure Decision on International Investment Incentives and Disincentives.[3]

All that had been achieved by that time was a recognition of 'the need to give due weight' to the interests of other countries that might be affected by one's investment policies with regard to multinational enterprises. The vague wording of the Decision in fact proclaimed loud and clear the very different view taken by the United States, on the one hand, and the European Community, on the other. The United States took the view that the Decision was meant to apply to any incentive or disincentive that directly or indirectly affected the international flow of investments, while according to the Community's interpretation it only applied to incentives or disincentives expressly applicable to foreign investments.[4]

This was already much less of an obligation than what is anyway contained in the GATT's Article XVI, where section B states that countries granting general production subsidies which operate 'directly or indirectly' to increase exports or reduce imports, and which cause or threaten to cause 'serious prejudice' to another member, must be prepared to discuss 'the possibility of limiting the subsidisation'.

Nevertheless, governments turned from the unsuccessful OECD forum to the more promising GATT forum in the hope that, in the Tokyo Round negotiations, the vague enough terms of Article XVI(B) might be improved upon and proper international guidelines on the extent of permissable subsidisation might be agreed upon.

The negotiating positions of the principal protagonists were far apart. The United States, taking a strict view of subsidisation, wished to establish a clear distinction between permissible, tolerated and prohibited subsidies, in exchange for which it was prepared to modify its domestic trade law which had led to the imposition of countervailing duties on Michelin tyres from Canada.

American trade law[5] differed from GATT rules in this respect. While the former provided for countervailing duties in respect of *any* subsidised product, whether or not it actually harmed local interests, the latter, in Article VI, permitted signatory countries to levy countervailing duties on subsidised goods only if they caused or threatened to cause domestic producers 'material injury'.[6] Thus the GATT, as it stood, was more lenient towards subsidisation than American law, which pre-dated the GATT[7] and hung like a sword of Damocles over the growing 'industrial policies' of Western Europe. It accordingly became a major negotiating objective of the European Community to persuade the United States to accept an 'injury' criterion in the assessment of its countervailing duties.[8]

The scene was therefore set for a balanced agreement: a clarification of the notion of subsidy, according to the three-fold classification suggested by the United States, in exchange for its acceptance of an 'injury' criterion. Such an agreement, ideally, would have reinforced the degree of international surveillance both over domestic subsidisation policies *and* over the introduction of countervailing duties in order to prevent the abuse of rights on both sides. In the event, the Code on Subsidies and Countervailing Duties, agreed in the Tokyo Round negotiations, appeared to increase international control over the introduction of countervailing duties, including the need to provide proof of 'injury', without any corresponding increase in international control over subsidisation policies *per se*. On the contrary, the European Community even managed to wring from the United States a recognition of 'the social utility of subsidy programs', which was certainly not what the United States originally set out to accomplish.

Thus the net effect of five years of hard work was to make it easier, rather than harder, to distort international trade flows with the help of domestic subsidies.

Another Example: Selective Safeguards

Another striking example of Western governments reacting to the problem of over-capacity in a defensive and inward-looking manner has related to the question of 'safeguards'. The European Community entered the Tokyo Round negotiations with the objective of securing the right to apply 'selective' safeguards; that is, the right to apply emergency import restrictions on a discriminatory basis against a sudden surge of imports of a particular product from an identifiable source. The argument can be put very persuasively. The GATT gives countries the right, under Article XIX, to take emergency safeguard action unilaterally if, 'as a result of unforeseen developments', imports cause or threaten to cause 'serious injury' to local producers. According to GATT rules, however, such emergency restrictions must apply to all imports, whatever their source. Why should everybody suffer, the Community argued, if only one country is the source of the problem? Selective safeguards would limit the impact of emergency measures and would therefore be less disruptive of trade. Another argument in favour of changing Article XIX, less widely proclaimed, was the fact that unilateral safeguard measures were extremely 'expensive' – countries availing themselves of this escape clause had to offer equivalent compensation, in the form of lower tariffs on other goods, to the injured trade partners. This, it was argued, made it harder for governments to agree to substantial tariff cuts which might possibly cause market disruption. The objective of the reform of Article XIX was to make emergency action easier: that is to say, 'cheaper', more legitimate and less disruptive, but subject to stricter international surveillance.

Another potent argument in favour of this proposed reform was the need to clean up the growing legal slum constituted by 'voluntary' export restraints and 'orderly marketing arrangements'. These were, in fact, selective safeguards negotiated bilaterally outside the GATT framework and usually in flagrant contradiction to the General Agreement. Since no one – not even a sovereign government – likes to be seen breaking the law, even international law, it became urgent to bring these arrangements into the GATT system by a judicious modification of Article XIX.

There are occasional half-hearted attempts to draw a useful distinction between 'voluntary' export restraints (unilateral action, on the part of an exporting country, supposedly not constituting an 'agreement' in violation of the GATT) and 'orderly marketing agreements' (bilateral agreements between governments or private trade associations). But in law the only useful distinction to be made is between, on the one hand, inter-governmental agreements to restrict trade, which are sovereign acts and constitute international law, however informal they may be, and are often in violation of the GATT, and, on the other hand, private agreements to restrict quantities and/or raise prices, which are generally null and void under the terms of anti-trust or anti-restrictive-practices legislation in most countries.

The most common type of selective trade restriction appears to take the form of an exchange of letters, whereby the trade ministry of the importing country, a developed country, kindly requests that the trade ministry of the exporting country should impress upon the relevant trade associations the need to keep export growth within 'reasonable' bounds, in the absence of which his government would regretfully have to envisage the possibility of taking unilateral safeguard action under Article XIX of the GATT. (The author has had access to letters such as these and, while being unable to quote them directly, can personally testify to their existence.) In his reply, the exporting country's trade minister acknowledges receipt of the letter, reiterates its contents and concludes with a polite farewell. Is this an agreement or is it not? According to John H. Jackson, of the University of Michigan, a leading legal authority in the field, such an exchange of notes establishes international obligations in the same way as a solemnly negotiated treaty: 'International agreements are not limited to those embodied in formal documents, authenticated with ceremony, but include . . . the specifying of an arrangement, together with mutual assurances and understandings as to how all parties will behave.'[9]

There is no way of assessing the total number of such agreements. Nor is there any way of assessing the amount of trade covered by them in an absolute sense. But a clear indication of their increased use after 1974 was given by Bahran Nowzad in a study for the IMF which listed the number of export measures applied by Taiwan, Columbia and South Korea from 1971 to 1977. According to these data, the accumulated number of export restraints applied by these three countries jumped from four in 1971–73 to 100 in 1974–77.[10]

Thus three arguments militated in favour of a reform of the GATT safeguard mechanism:

   (a) to make safeguard action less disruptive than under Article XIX;

   (b) to make safeguard action 'cheaper' in order to incite governments to more daring tariff offers; and

   (c) to clean up the legal slum of 'orderly marketing arrangements'.

The price asked of the United States was its acceptance of the principle of discrimination – as opposed to the principle of non-discrimination which has been the cornerstone of the GATT system – in the use of safeguards, while what the European Community was prepared to pay was acceptance of closer international surveillance of the use of safeguard measures. Agreement was in fact reached on this basis, and the document was ready for signature in time for the umpteenth 'final' Tokyo Round meeting just before the Easter of 1979 when, at the eleventh hour, the developing countries – possibly inspired by an outwardly calm and inscrutable, but doubtless inwardly worried, Japan and also Australia and Canada – announced that they would not countenance the selective safeguard code. Since the developed countries could not muster anywhere near the necessary two-thirds majority needed to amend the GATT (Article XXX) the whole code was thrown back into the melting pot. It was all too easy for a country to say, 'my tariff offer only holds good if the selective safeguard clause is signed'. The European Community went one step further and announced that it intended to apply the selective safeguard code unilaterally. It followed this up with open threats to restrict Japanese trade by the end of 1979 if Japan refused to take appropriate measures to reduce her trade surplus with the European Community and even leaked an extraordinary internal paper accusing the Japanese of being 'workaholics' and disrupting world trade by their refusal to consume.[11]

Five years of painstaking negotiation, far from bringing about a meeting of minds, simply served to crystallise the differences. On this particular issue, however, a meeting of minds would have been disastrous and the demise of the proposed selective safeguard code had to be greeted with a sigh of relief. Why?

As suggested earlier, the case for selective safeguards is persuasive. It seems so *sensible* to limit the effect of emergency action to one or two countries. What could be more attractive than to enjoy all the benefits of international trade and specialisation without the aggravation of 'market disruption'?

The answer, quite simply, is that the two cannot be disassociated. Unless one is prepared to live with the perpetual structural shifts caused by competition with efficient producers the world over, one cannot expect to reap the benefits of international trade, which are the greater, the larger are the international relative price differences. It is an illusion to believe that one can enjoy the gains from trade for nothing.

As for discriminatory safeguards in particular, three good reasons can be advanced against them – one legal, one economic and one political.

The legal argument is in two steps. To amend the GATT to permit discriminatory safeguards would open the flood-gates of discrimination in all kinds of circumstances. It would fundamentally alter the nature of the GATT system which, as already mentioned, is based on the principle of non-discrimination expressed in Article I, which requires most-favoured-nation, or 'equal', treatment to be accorded unconditionally to all signatory countries. Well, one might argue, why not? The GATT and multilateral trade negotiations have had a good innings. Is it not time to change? But the legal grounds for preferring non-discrimination to discrimination are that the former system protects small and weak countries from the abuse of power by large and strong ones. In a discriminatory trading system, market access is not a right, to be earned through competition and excellence, but is up for grabs through arm-twisting, blackmail and favouritism.

Decisions which should normally be taken on commercial grounds become the object of political trade-offs. In such a system, small countries, without bargaining counters, are unprotected. Since it is one purpose of the law to protect the weak from the abuse of power by the strong, such a trade system would not constitute a proper legal order, but a reversion to the law of the jungle.

In economic terms, discrimination permits countries to penalise the most disruptive (that is, efficient) producers in the world. This is a retreat from the GATT position which, while not being one of free trade (first-best optimum), nevertheless offers a second-best optimum: although domestic producers are favoured over foreigners, the latter can compete with each other on an equal footing for a part of the domestic market. Discrimination, by penalising the most efficient producers, directly reduces world income and will ultimately also reduce real incomes in the countries applying the safeguards.

In political terms, discrimination, by allowing countries to treat other nations differently one from the other, offers endless cause for friction and discontent. Even the non-discriminatory system, as it is supposed to be, has not been proof against trade disputes which have come very close to trade wars or at least skirmishes (viz. the notorious 'chicken war' of 1963, in the name of which the United States took retaliatory measures against French cognac – the removal of which was offered as a conciliatory gesture as part of the final Tokyo Round 'package'). A discriminatory legal system, crowned by a discredited GATT, would be unable to prevent a serious dispute from deteriorating because there would be no clear guidelines on how to react in given circumstances. In a way, one would almost be spoiling for a fight, but we are not there yet, although we are closer to a discriminatory trading system than we have ever been since the 1930s.

Deterioration of the International Trading System

Why should the deterioration of the international trading system have occurred? To some, this might seem a rather naive question, for there is an obvious, although somewhat superficial, answer: the developed West European economies are incapable of accepting change at anything like the pace which is currently being demanded of them. Change is crowding in from all quarters – the increased price of energy, brave new worlds opened up by the fascinating and horrible 'chip' and, on top of all this, an unstemmable flood of cheap and desirable goods from youthful and dynamic 'workaholic' countries like Japan, South Korea, Taiwan, Hong Kong and Singapore. Since Western Europe or, more specifically, the European Community cannot affect the price of oil, nor stem the sudden flood of new technology, let it at least act on one controllable item, namely trade. That, indeed, is what the Community has done and the decision-making process is probably no more complicated than that.

What shocks an economist, however, is the knowledge that by acting instinctively in this way, the governments of the European Community are storing up far greater trouble for the future and will, in fact, accentuate the Community's problem of coping with change rather than assuage it. The arguments are well known, simple and logically irrefutable.

One Argument

If a country limits its imports it inevitably reduces its exports. This is because by restricting its imports, it reduces other countries' exports, hence their incomes, hence their demand for our country's exports. It may take a bit of time for these effects to work themselves out, but this is how it will go, because world exports are tautologically equal to world imports and a reduction of the one implies, necessarily, a reduction of the other. One could argue that our country might, by beggar-thy-neighbour policies, at least temporarily maintain its share of world exports while reducing its share of world imports, but this position would be undermined by an unwanted but irresistible exchange-rate appreciation or a rise in the internal price level, compared with the former period, either of which would re-establish the previous competitive position at a lower level of trade all around.

In other words, jobs saved in the import-competing sector are, sooner rather than later, lost in the export sector and nothing is gained. Rather, the jobs which would have been lost in the import-competing sector (by definition in an area where our country is losing comparative advantage) have instead been lost in the export sector (which by definition is the area where resources should be concentrated). We are therefore compromising our long-term future for 'overriding political considerations' or, more precisely, for the understandable anxiety of Mr Member-of-Parliament to be re-elected and Mr X to keep his current job and level of earnings.

Another Argument

Even if a country has unemployed resources, in the form of idle machines and idle workers, the above argument still holds.

This is because, in modern times, no country need suffer from an absence of effective demand. If there are genuinely idle resources that could be brought into productive use at the drop of a governmental penny, one can rest assured that this would be done.

The sad fact is, however, that over-capacity in both capital and labour resources is not due to a lack of effective demand. A simple test of this proposition is to imagine what would happen if the government increased its budget deficit in order to 'mop it up'. Would production increase or would inflation rise? Almost certainly the latter would happen.

Therefore, the high rates of over-capacity that began to develop in the 1970s have been structural: they have reflected both the frictional minimum needed to accomplish the transition from an industrial to a service economy and structural imperfections in the labour market. In a sense, they do not constitute usable resources at all. As far as plant and machinery are concerned, much of it was rendered economically useless as a result of the rise in oil prices, away back in 1973. Firms have continued to carry useless capital equipment on their books because they have not wanted to take the capital loss right on the nose. But in fact it should be scrapped. Byegones should be byegones in evaluating capital goods.

People who were employed to operate energy-intensive capital equipment or who have skills in energy-intensive activities (such as steel-making and other metal making) or who are being replaced by robots have similarly lost their economic use and can only regain it if they adapt their skills to the needs of the market (if the trade unions will let them). An adult with several years of education and work experience behind him or her is a highly capital-intensive resource and runs the risk that this investment might be depreciated overnight by a malicious twist of market fortunes. History is full of examples, from the wheelwright to the bus conductor (who quaintly survives in the United Kingdom, but not, to my knowledge, anywhere else).

Society as a whole can, and does, cushion the shock, but it cannot turn the clock back. We presumably owe it to ourselves to manage our capital as best we can and remain alert to changes in demand for it – which, after all, have a good chance of being opportunities rather than threats. But until the need for change is accepted by those who, through no fault of their own, suddenly experience a depreciation in the value of their own human capital, they remain intrinsically unemployable, except at a wage which reflects the capital loss. No amount of tariff protection can cope with changes of this nature.

. . . and Another

If a country limits imports of intermediate goods, it renders all user industries down-stream less competitive and, therefore, threatens a multitude of jobs even more directly. This, for instance, is the case of steel, where the European-Community's Davignon Plan succeeded in raising steel prices by 50 per cent in 1978. There are some nine million workers in the Common Market's steel-using industries as opposed to some 750 000 in the steel industry proper. Who can say how many down-stream jobs have been sacrificed for those up-stream?

. . . and One More

Whatever happens, import limitations raise prices. These reduce real incomes and there is less to spend on other things. The whole economy grows more slowly and the growth of 'other' sectors is stifled. Yet it is 'other things' which represent the future. It is these which would provide the alternative occupations for Mr X if they were given the chance to expand. But since protection limits their potential expansion, their sluggish growth will soon confirm the dire predictions of the 'market failure' hypothesis, whereby the free market is incapable of offering alternative employment to Mr X. Confronted with a sluggish, slow or even negative growth economy, the predictable policy response will be for more protection, not less, and the vicious circle will continue down to the next level.

Thus an initial reaction to over-capacity in an industry, based on simplistic and partial equilibrium grounds, on governmental lack of nerve and on genuine concern for the victims of the market fluctuation at the back of the whole problem, leads to an aggravation of the initial situation, which in turn calls forth the same erroneous policy response, which meets with the same predictable lack of success, which leads to the reinforcement of past erroneous policies and so on. The question is how many circles must be experienced before the validity of the protectionist response is questioned. The answer, I believe, is a great many.

Why? Partly because of ignorance. People do not believe that they are in any way affected by protectionism. And partly because collective capacity for clear thinking is clouded by two very human emotions. First, people's sense of justice is offended when they see other people who, through no fault of their own, lose their job or suffer a reversal of their economic fortunes.[12] Secondly, there is in people a little niggling fear that perhaps this nasty blind force, called the market, might pick them out as its next victims. Therefore, even if people at present enjoy the favours of the market, they on the whole support the idea of some form of collective insurance against the risks to which it exposes them. Thus protectionism can be interpreted as the collectivisation of market risk by society and an attempt to find security from it albeit at a lower level of income.

Sadly, however, people cannot expect to enjoy the benefits of the market without running the risks as well. It is perhaps symptomatic of ageing populations that people seem, collectively, to prefer a safe existence at a low standard of living to a risky one at a high level of income. Lest anybody should suffer the illusion that the trade-off is trivial in real terms, consider for a moment the cost, in the form of lost income, of a policy which raises the domestic price of tradeable goods by 50 per cent above the world's lowest-cost producer (not an unrealistic assumption if one looks at the European Community's common agricultural policy or its Davignon Plan). In any typical advanced West European country, people spend about 20 per cent of their disposable income on food, 5 per cent on drink and tobacco, 5–7 per cent on clothing and textiles, 5 per cent on automobiles and household equipment, the remainder going on heating, light, transport, health, sport, education and entertainment. Thus about 35 per cent of current household expenditure (on food, drink, clothing, furniture and gadgets) is on goods in principle exposable to world market prices. If prices are 50 per cent above world market levels, it means that consumers in the Community are transferring about 11.7 per cent of their real disposable incomes to producers by way of higher prices. This is not a mere innocuous transfer from a less deserving segment of the population to a more meritorious one. It constitutes a net loss overall, because the same needs could have been satisfied at a third of the cost in real resource terms.

Are people really prepared to pay such a high premium for insurance against the risk of market fluctuations? I can already hear the 'ayes'! But in all fairness it must be added that one cannot guarantee water-tight shelter from market risk. For instance, fluctuations in market fortunes can come from changes in technology and tastes, from natural disasters, against which the highest tariff in the world cannot protect one. So, in their search for security, people are sacrificing a potentially large slice of real income in exchange for a rather leaky vessel. But people might be prepared to accept this bargain if they placed a very high value on security and a relatively low value on income. This is the case of very wealthy and security-conscious societies and, if one could be sure of maintaining present levels of real income into the future, many people would be satisfied. This, however, is impossible in an area, namely the European Community, which depends on other areas for 80 per cent of its oil and 75 per cent of its raw materials. There are many and growing contenders for these precious commodities and they will be allocated in the future, as in the past, to the highest bidders. It will be no use going to the auctions of the future without very well-lined pockets and the money will have to be earned the usual hard way, by exporting, and this will not be easy if the people of the Community have decided to shelter themselves from the fluctuations of the market. They shall have to trade as the East European countries do, without reference to real costs, just in order to buy essential food and raw materials. This is not wealth. It is extreme poverty.

In short, I see a great danger of self-perpetuating impoverishment because of the natural and understandable but naïve reaction of people to the problem of unemployment. That this problem is not caused solely by imports is obvious, but trade is the only variable that governments can act upon, apparently without hurting any specific domestic interests. In the meantime, some of the obstacles to the free exercise of sovereign power in trade matters, carefully built up in the years of prosperity, are in the process of being washed away. There is no point in lamenting their disappearance. They will be ignored as long as governments fail to see the long-term implications of current trends and to realise that protection and discrimination are games in which the protectionists lose most.

Once this is recognised, and governments revert of their own volition to open trade and monetary policies, the present perceived conflict between national economic interests and international economic ties will evaporate. Indeed, economics suggests that it is a spurious conflict, since national economic interests are served, and served well, by open economic policies. In these circumstances a single conference will be sufficient to restore the foundations of a viable international economic order.

NOTES

1. This chapter is based on an article by the author, 'Surplus Capacity and What the Tokyo Round Failed to Settle', *The World Economy*, London, September 1979, an earlier version having been presented at a conference of the International Political Economy Group on 'The Management of Surplus Capacity in the 1970s' held at Cumberland Lodge, Windsor, in the United Kingdom, on 2–4 May 1979.

2. The General Agreement was negotiated in 1947 and entered into force in January 1948. The twenty three countries which originally signed it were at the time engaged in drawing up the charter for a proposed International Trade Organisation (ITO) which would have been a United Nations specialised agency. The General Agreement, based largely on selected parts of the draft ITO charter, was concluded in order to get trade liberalisation under way quickly and was provided with only minimum institutional arrangements because it was expected that responsibility for it would soon be assumed by the ITO. Plans for the ITO had to be abandoned, however, when it became clear that its charter would not be ratified, particularly by the Congress of the United States. Thus the General Agreement was left as the only international instrument laying down trade rules accepted by nations responsible for most of the world's trade.

3. Henri Schwamm and Dimitri Germidis, *Codes of Conduct for Multinational Companies: Issues and Problems* (Brussels: ECSIM, 1977) p. 33.

4. *Ibid.,* p. 36.

5. The American law providing for countervailing import duties goes back to 1893.

6. Puzzled by what this term meant a lawyer in the United States

Treasury was heard to presume it to mean 'non-spiritual' injury.

7. Because of the 'grandfather clause' in the General Agreement the American law took precedence over GATT rules.

8. For a succinct analysis of the issues, see Harald B. Malmgren, *International Order for Public Subsidies*, Thames Essay No. 11 (London: Trade Policy Research Centre, 1977).

9. John H. Jackson, *Legal Problems of International Economic Relations* (St Paul, Minnesota: West Publishing, 1977) p. 105.

10. Bahran Nowzad, *The Rise in Protectionism* (Washington: International Monetary Fund, 1978).

11. The report, prepared by Sir Roy Denman, as Director-General for External Affairs in the Commission of the European Community, was 'leaked' to the press. See, for example, *The Economist*, London, 7 April 1979.

12. See F. A. Hayek, *The Road to Serfdom*, abridged edition (London: Routledge, 1946) p. 63.

The passage referred to describes the current situation so aptly that it deserves to be quoted in full: 'That anybody should suffer a great diminution of his income and bitter disappointment of all his hopes through no fault of his own, and despite hard work and exceptional skill, undoubtedly offends our sense of justice. The demands of those who suffer in this way, for state interference on their behalf to safeguard their legitimate expectations, are certain to receive popular sympathy and support. The general approval of these demands has had the effect that governments everywhere have taken action, not merely to protect the people so threatened from severe hardship and privation, but to secure to them the continued receipt of their former income and to shelter them from fluctuations of the market, that is of supply and demand.'

CHAPTER TWO

Industrial Policy, the Market and the State

In Chapter 1 has been briefly sketched the global context in which the debate over industrial policies in developed countries has been getting under way. Industrial policies in Western Europe, especially in the countries of the European Community, have been drawing most of the fire, particularly from the United States and, increasingly, the more advanced of the developing countries against whose exports of manufactures the corresponding industries in developed countries are finding it hard to compete.

Industrial policy may be generally defined as any government measure, or set of measures, to promote or prevent structural change. In this broad sense, mature market-oriented economies, in the industrialised world, have had industrial policies for a very long time. For instance, they have without exception, and with little if any intermission in the recent and even distant past, distorted market signals by means of differentiated tariffs. These establish a system of incentives and disincentives which affect the pattern of industrial production and the allocation of resources. By deciding on the relative supply of public goods, such as health, education, communications and defence, governments also affect the structure of industry. Even by changing income distribution through transfers, governments affect demand and, hence, industrial structure. In this broad sense, then, industrial policy is nothing new (it might be deemed synonymous with trade policy) and forms part of the traditional attributes of government, namely defence against outside aggression, enforcement of private contracts and maintenance of order within society and, too, the provision of public goods.

Reasons for Modern Industrial Policies

There has developed in recent years, however, a new attribute of government which is industrial policy in a narrower sense and which can be defined as any *selective* government measure, or set of measures, to prevent or promote structural change *on a specific ad hoc basis*. Thus modern industrial policy aims at more than merely setting a general framework. It descends increasingly into the microeconomic sphere of economic decision taking that was formerly left to the price mechanism.

There are two basic types of industrial policy – whether broadly or narrowly defined. One is positive and forward looking: its aim is to assist the process of structural change either by promoting new industries and high technology or by helping old ones to 'restructure'. The other is negative: it attempts to slow down, or even prevent, the process of structural change or, more bluntly, to keep declining sectors alive through artificial respiration. The basic social purpose served by positive industrial policy is clear. It is intended to raise productivity, maintain competitiveness and, thereby, secure a higher standard of living for people than might otherwise have been the case. Whether or not it actually succeeds in achieving these objectives is another question.

The social purpose served by negative industrial policy, however, is more ambiguous. Like the tariff, it raises incomes in the protected industry, to the detriment of other members of society. This is politically acceptable only because the transfer is made from a very large number of people to the very few, so that a small per capita contribution makes a very great difference to recipients' incomes. But society must bear an additional burden: by keeping resources locked up in declining sectors, negative industrial policy *reduces* national income below what it would have been in its absence.

Indeed, one must seek non-economic justifications for negative industrial policy, the most frequently cited being the need to save jobs and to avoid social and political tensions arising from an abrupt loss of viability in a particular sector. Even more than in the case of positive industrial policy, it is an open question whether negative industrial policy really achieves its stated non-economic objectives. Can social harmony truly be promoted by policies which reduce national income?

The answer is 'no' – in the long run. Even so, a mixture of perfectly understandable human emotions, ranging from compassion for the victims of market fluctuation to fear of loss of public office on the part of elected representatives, leads to the adoption of negative industrial policies in the short run. This short-term policy trap is particularly dangerous because it fosters inefficiency, thus creating exactly the negative type of economic environment in which more negative industrial policies will flourish.

A common factor linking both types of industrial policy is a lack of public confidence in private entrepreneurial ability, either to seize on the opportunities offered by new industries, or to move fast enough to save old ones. Rather than rely on that rather mythical creature, the entrepreneur, modern governments, faced with large structural changes and potentially heavy job-losses, prefer to take matters into their own hands.

The neat distinction between positive and negative industrial policy often becomes blurred in practice not least because governments are permanently torn between economic efficiency and political expediency and will try to steer a middle course. The resolution of this conflict is perhaps the key to a successful industrial policy.

Before exploring this aspect of the question, however, is seems appropriate to discuss the reasons behind the recent expansion of industrial policies in Western Europe.

Academic Argument

A respectable body of academic opinion provides ample justification for selective government intervention in the economy, arising from such critics of the market system as Joan Robinson, of the University of Cambridge, and John Kenneth Galbraith, of Harvard University. In the 'structuralist' thesis, perfect or near-perfect markets are the exceptions. In these situations, the invisible hand is conspicuous mainly by its absence and the state is needed to supplement market forces, such as they are, and replace them altogether if necessary. Even those who believe that the structuralists have gone too far, and who acknowledge that large firms compete fiercely (if imperfectly) with each other, may advocate government action to improve the market mechanism and help cope with the uncertainties of the future.

A good modern and very fair exponent of these ideas is James

Meade, the British economist, who was awarded the Nobel prize for economics in 1978. According to Professor Meade,

> the intelligent radical will support the restoration and development of the free market mechanism wherever it is possible to ensure competitive conditions [because] the great virtue of the competitive market mechanism is that it combines efficiency with freedom . . . *But he recognises that on the foundation of this market mechanism there must be built a superstructure of governmental interventions and controls.*[1]

One of the main questions that divide contemporary economists is where the free market should end and the 'superstructure of governmental interventions and controls' should begin. Some people draw the frontier in such a way that the role reserved for the market is as large as possible, thus minimising the role of the state, while others do the opposite. Where one draws the line depends partly on whether one believes that modern industrial structures generate enough competitive forces spontaneously to guarantee a reasonably efficient allocation of resources in private goods markets, or not, and partly on some fundamental political attitudes.

The first question is a mixture of positive and normative economics. It ought to be a question which could be settled solely with an appeal to fact. Is there enough competition or is there not? Is private entrepreneurship dead or is it alive? But exactly how much evidence one needs to be convinced either way is a matter of personal judgement and gives rise to a normative quarrel over what is basically a positive issue.

The political aspect of the matter, which revolves around the threat to individual liberty due to the steady expansion of government in economic affairs, is clearly normative and can only be settled (among reasonable people) by an agreement to disagree. Some would be prepared to take the risk of leaving the economy in the hands of imperfect entrepreneurs, as an alternative to the even greater risk of having it run by imperfect government, while others take the opposite view.

When drawing one's personal frontier between the state and the market one will have to decide on which side to put the vexed question of structural adaptation – a truly borderline case. Can the market be entrusted with this task or is there a 'need for the central planning of large structural changes in the economy'?[2] The middle-of-the-road position, taken by Professor Meade, is that the market can cope with marginal structural change, but that it needs help when it comes to major structural upheavals. A more interventionist note is struck in an article in the *National Westminster Bank Quarterly Review* by D. L. Hodgson who believes that 'government has an important part to play in helping industry achieve a better overall performance' . . . either by direct means (nationalisation) or by indirect means (subsidies, incentives or whatever),[3] while S. C. Littlechild, of the University of Birmingham, in an essay for the Institute of Economic Affairs in London, remains deeply sceptical: 'In a world of uncertainty, national plans and planning agreements can achieve coordination only at the expense of freedom to initiate and response to change. Far from supplementing the market process, national planning precludes it.'[4]

Whatever views one may hold, however, it is an objective fact that the debate itself has provided many arguments which can be used to justify direct and indirect state intervention in the economy to promote or prevent structural change; and it is both unsurprising and indubitable that many governments in advanced industrial countries should have availed themselves of them.

Replacement of Tariffs by Industrial Policy

In previous decades, as mentioned above, the principal instrument of industrial policy was the tariff. But the tariff is now obsolete. All industrial market-oriented economies are signatories to the GATT, the instrument by which international trade has been regulated since the end of World War II, and most of them have 'bound' their tariffs in successive 'rounds' of multilateral trade negotiations aimed at liberalising commerce. Members of the European Community have even surrendered their right to use tariffs to a supranational body, namely the Commission of the Community, based in Brussels. Tariffs, therefore, cannot be used freely to promote this or that industry and, as a result, governments are forced back onto non-tariff measures of various kinds, including outright subsidies. There is little doubt that the very success of past efforts to liberalise international trade has led to the substitution of tariffs by other measures with equivalent effects[5] and has contributed to the development *inter alia* of micro-economic industrial policies.

Internationalisation of Business

The development of multinational enterprises, which not only leap over tariffs with ease, but are actually stimulated to do so the higher they are, has made customs duties useless as instruments for the encouragement of specific *national* industries. However much governments may welcome foreign direct investments for macro-economic reasons, they begin to worry if local firms in what are considered to be 'key-sectors' are non-existent, disappear or lose ground. Government aid to specific national firms is the only answer.

Computers offer a classical example of the uselessness of tariffs in encouraging a locally-owned, modern, high-technology industry. Any tariff on computers in the European Community high enough to bring a European computer industry into existence in the 1960s would have simultaneously attracted a great deal of direct investment by American computer manufacturers which, in turn, would have cancelled out the protective effect of the tariff. In the 1960s, France, Germany and Britain therefore all adopted broadly similar industrial policies to establish their respective national computer industries. They (i) encouraged mergers, (ii) provided straight grants for research and development to the newly-formed 'national champions' and (iii) reserved for them the government 'market' for computers.[6] The great advantage of this policy – apart from offering national champions real protection – was not to raise the price of computers to other private firms which remained free to buy machines at world prices. Thus foreign direct investment, by undermining the protective impact of tariffs and rendering them obsolete, forced on governments the use of a superior instrument of industrial policy – namely, the selective, outright subsidy.

The Recession

The 'recession', or the slowdown in growth in the world economy, which began in earnest in 1975 and which has proved to be the deepest and longest since Keynesian demand-management policies were first introduced after World War II, has provided two more reasons for the growing use of industrial policy in Western Europe.

Governments have been faced with the novel and contradictory combination of inflation and stagnation. With the familiar box of Keynesian policy tools, they could not fight the one without aggravating the other. Britain and Italy fought stagnation and reaped only inflation. Germany and Switzerland fought inflation, successfully, but reaped stagnation. After an initial period of trial and error, most governments ended up fighting inflation with macro-economic tools; and fighting the resulting stagnation with industrial policy.

Also the very severity of the recession meant that the number of industries 'in difficulty' grew alarmingly. To begin with most governments provided stop-gap aid to prevent large-scale bankruptcies (and their ensuing chain-reaction endangering otherwise viable creditor firms). The principal objective was to preserve employment through the trough of the recession until expansion got under way again. Thus cyclical job-preservation was added to the traditional list of objectives to be achieved by industrial policy. But it soon became clear that many firms faced structural rather than cyclical difficulties and that what started out as a temporary policy was in danger of becoming permanent.

The implications of extending automatic stop-gap help to firms facing structural decline are only too obvious: *inter alia* they will progressively drain the viable industries of resources, rendering them candidates for the emergency ward as well. This is gradually dawning on West European governments and a distinct change of emphasis is discernable. The days when Mr Boussac could, with his 11 000 employees, be assured of the French Government's support in the name of job preservation are almost over; and the Government furthermore seems to be persevering in its plans to rationalise the steel industry despite violent opposition from the labour force. Even in the United Kingdom the Labour Government of James Callaghan went ahead with the closure of several high-cost steel works, shutting its ears to the anguished cries of the trade unions. Thus, much as governments may be moved by short-run considerations and wish to avoid at all cost the painful process of structural adjustment, if the change is very large they are virtually forced to submit to it. The result will be industrial policies to reduce the pace of structural change, but not to stop it altogether. This involves the measured 'rationalisation' of declining industries, a hybrid of positive and negative industrial policies.

Challenges from Developing Countries and Technological Change

This brings us to two further reasons for the sudden renewal of interest in industrial policy: competition from highly efficient (or subsidised) and low-cost producers in Japan, Eastern Europe and newly industrialising countries of the Third World; and the prospect of a major industrial change due to the 'micro-processor revolution'. These structural challenges would be significant enough taken singly; together, they are monumental. Furthermore, they are interconnected and therefore reinforce each other. Briefly stated, the problem is to make West European industry competitive with, say, South Korea, at West European wage levels. Impossible? Not at all! But it does imply substituting capital for labour on a large scale. The search for machines to do people's jobs is on – and the market has a solution to hand, the micro-processor. Without dire competition from newly industrialising countries and the countries of Eastern Europe, however, the introduction of micro-processors might have taken years. As it is, a major leap in productivity, comparable perhaps in its implications with the invention of steam-power, is being squeezed into the space of a few short years. The point is that governments can protect industry from foreign competition, *but not from technological change*, which can often prove infinitely more disruptive of established interests. In any event, it is clear to all concerned that many West European industries will be shedding labour at an unprecedented rate over the 1980s in order to remain competitive internationally and keep their remaining workers in the style to which they are accustomed. What happens to those dismissed in the process?

Faced with such large, as opposed to marginal, structural changes, who would dispute the need for government planning to smooth the process of adaptation, guide it in the right direction and see to it that unemployment does not get out of hand? Politicians of various persuasions, civil servants, industrialists, trade unions, economists and, indeed, the public are virtually united on this point. It is therefore hardly surprising that the state should have risen magnificently to the occasion by expanding the arsenal of industrial policies. Unfortunately, whatever responsibilities electorates thrust upon the state, one thing is sure: those responsibilities will never be returned to them. People, collectively and individually, are accordingly rushing down a one-way street and it is high time they took stock of the situation.

What is at Stake?

The academic debate on where to draw the boundary line between the state and the market is usually conducted in strictly economic terms, such as market failure or the socialisation of risk. While there is much to be said in defence of markets, even oligopolistic ones, and much to be said in praise of risk as a stimulant to human action, the debate cannot be resolved on these grounds alone. Arguments showing the material efficiency of markets as opposed to governments will either tend to be disputed by the true believers in the structural thesis or, if accepted, will be deemed irrelevent, since man does not live by bread alone.

Generations of economists, for instance, have demonstrated beyond reasonable doubt that tariffs diminish national income, yet protection continues to flourish, supported not only by the vested interests directly concerned but also by the population at large, as a sovereign remedy for economic ills. The appeal to material efficiency simply cuts no ice, has not done so for two centuries and shows no signs of doing so in the future. Moreover, after two centuries, it cannot be a question of education. Thus, too, with industrial policy. The government may be less efficient than the market in producing the goods that society wants, but at least it expresses a collective will to escape human bondage to 'impersonal' market forces. (That this impersonal mechanism in fact expresses society's collective economic will, and not some mysterious and unidentified inhuman influence, is overlooked or simply labelled 'wrong'.)

One of the worst offences of the market system is that it changes constantly, forcing on security-loving humanity an unacceptable pace of change. Much of the argument in favour of industrial policy, or for protection for that matter, stems from this collective craving for security, which is surely one of the few permanent main-springs of human action and which must have inspired our physically ill-equipped primitive forebears to develop their intellectual powers instead of their bone and muscle. In the present incomparably more comfortable industrial jungle, the urge for security is as pressing as ever. Nowadays, however, threats to security take the form of market fluctuations, the normal human response to which is not to forge tools to overcome them, but to ask governments to provide a shelter from them – an apparently least-cost avenue which was not open to our ancestors.

There are two distinct costs involved in such a choice. First, a person cannot expect to enjoy the benefits of the market system without running some of the risks. If the risk is eliminated, so is the income associated with it. (This, though, is an example of a material argument with little appeal in a wealthy and security-conscious society.) Secondly, even if individuals refuse to bear them, risks themselves will not go away. They will have to be borne collectively by the state and how will the state insure itself? The answer is only too obvious. By leaving a minimum to chance – that is, to individual decision-takers. Thus the craving for security leads inexorably away from freedom, as surely as domestic animals are enticed into bondage. This is the major and, in my view, irrefutable argument against entrusting the state with responsibility to shelter society from change, even from major structural upheavals which may cause a great deal of individual hardship.

Lest this last sentence should seem excessively harsh, let it be immediately stated that unemployment insurance, income supplements and generous redundancy payments are all perfectly compatible with market-induced industrial change. Indeed, they represent an excellent way of spreading the risks of market fluctuations throughout society without actually stopping the fluctuations themselves. What is not compatible with market-oriented industrial change and, ultimately, individual liberty is systematic occupational insurance, on the one hand, and structural change directed by the state, on the other. Thus, even if it could be demonstrated that governments could help the process of structural adaptation by specific *ad hoc* interventions (which is doubtful for reasons given below), the cost in terms of loss of liberty would be too high. Both sides can play at the game of going beyond material considerations and the clinching arguments still rest with the market mechanism.

Equity versus Efficiency

Combining economic efficiency with political expediency (or equity if one wishes to take a high moral tone) means taking account of people's perfectly legitimate concerns regarding their jobs and their incomes, without blunting the edge of the ruthless market process – a seemingly impossible task. Certainly, positive industrial policy in Western Europe does not take this form; rather, it blunts the edge of market forces to the degree thought necessary to slow the pace of structural change down to what is socially acceptable. If the source of change is import competition due to a change in tariff policy, 'adjustment assistance' is made available. If the purpose is to revitalise a dying sector, 'restructuring' is the password. In either case, public funds are provided to stave off collapse, but are made conditional on a 'restructuring plan'. This hybrid of positive and negative industrial policies is the best that governments have been able to devise. Only in Japan can one find examples of state action to *speed up* the process of structural change[7] – not a policy likely to recommend itself in Western Europe!

Trade liberalisation coupled with adjustment assistance is a typical example of the West European capacity for moving forwards while looking backwards. The justification in this case is that firms are subjected to a discontinuity of government policy and therefore deserve compensation. Yet this quite clearly cancels out part of the efficiency-promoting impact of the tariff cut.

Is there a way out of the dilemma? Can one devise a policy which meets the demands of equity (or expediency) *without* blunting the edge of economic efficiency? A policy which neither accelerates nor retards the speed of change, but which is politically acceptable?

Such a policy exists. It entails giving lump-sum state-financed compensation to employees who have lost their jobs because of a change in market circumstances, but not to firms as such. In this way, most of the people bearing the cost of adjustment would receive compensation from the public at large and most legitimate social concerns would be met. On the other hand, entrepreneurs – or their modern equivalents, top managers – would not be sheltered from market risk. They would suffer considerable loss of income and status if their firm were to fail and would therefore have every incentive to remain alert to market change and, if necessary, would not hesitate to avail themselves of the social safety net for their employees if market circumstances required reduced manning levels.

From the efficiency point of view, the economy's natural capacity for spontaneous structural change would not be stifled by the feather-bedding of business. Inefficiency would not be rewarded; and resistance to change combined with public funds would not exist as a rational and least-cost alternative to difficult and costly adjustment problems.

As for equity considerations, there seems to be considerable justice in providing compensation for loss of work to shop-floor employees (who, after all, are not expected to keep an eye on market developments or exercise a leadership role) and in withholding it from firms and their responsible management, whose claim to a position of leadership rests on their ability to anticipate change and react to it, if possible correctly.[8] Left to itself, a properly functioning stock market will, by and large, eliminate the consistently poor decision-takers through take-overs, usually before bankruptcy looms. All the same, a combination of well-intentioned merger regulations and job-preservation subsidies will (indeed *has* in many countries) reduced the stock market's culling function to negligible proportions.

Why should compensation take the form of a lump sum financed by the state? The main argument in favour of lump-sum compensation is that it encourages both entrepreneurship and adjustment. Not only will some of those compensated use their capital sum to start a business of their own, but most of the others will try to save rather than spend it. Thus the social compensation for adjustment will be recycled by the banking system back into the adjustment process itself, in the form of cheaper and more abundant capital for growing sectors of the economy. Why should compensation be financed by the long-suffering taxpayer, and not by the firm undertaking the restructuring process? The argument for this has become apparent in the light of experience. It is often forgotten that laws imposing upon firms the duty to provide severance pay and lump-sum compensation for loss of work were originally intended to *help* the process of restructuring, by making it easier for people to move from one job to another. In fact, as is now well known, the policy backfired, in that firms not only retained surplus labour as a lesser evil to the costs of dismissal, but studiously refrained from engaging new employees unless absolutely forced to do so. The result was less structural adjustment and above-average youth unemployment. In order to avoid these pitfalls, compensation needs to be provided by society at large – as is right and proper if it is considered that society as a whole benefits from easing the process of change.

It is often argued that state aid is due to a firm if it is the victim of a sudden change in government policy – in the United States, Chrysler's plea in 1979 for federal aid, for instance, was based on the difficulty it had in meeting an allegedly insurmountable combination of strict emission standards and stringent mileage norms. This is a difficult issue. Clearly, there is a measure of luck (or lack of it) when a totally unpredictable switch in government policy eliminates the very basis of a company's business. But unpredictable and/or discontinuous change is the very stuff of modern management. The market itself provides many equally devastating changes, in the form of technological progress, relative price shifts or fickle tastes. Keeping an eye on the whims of government policy is just one more complication. There is no obvious reason why this particular source of change should be compensated for and not the others. Moreover, the cost of compensating for all changes of government policy would be prohibitive, while an attempt to be selective would give rise to endless wrangling. It is therefore wiser to consider that adapting to changes in public policy fall within the normal mandate of a modern management team.

One last social partner remains to be discussed – the shareholder. Should he, she or it receive compensation for the loss of asset value due to a change in market fortunes or in public policy? The answer is 'no'. Shareholders should be given every incentive to channel their savings to growing sectors of the economy, which need capital, and away from declining sectors, which do not; they will remain alert to change only if they run the risk of losing their investments.

'Market Failure' as a Justification for Subsidies

If, without being able to point to a sudden change in government policies, tastes or technology, an industry has been losing ground for several years, if its capital stock is ancient, if its work force is unmotivated, if its plant is dirty and needs a coat of paint and if it has a generally run-down appearance, the casual on-looker or concerned civil servant is tempted to decide that all it needs is a once-and-for-all injection of capital and possibly a change of management. The underlying assumption is that the firm is a victim of 'market failure' – in other words, that the market has failed to place a correct 'social' value on the firm and has unjustly starved it of resources. This confuses cause and effect. Activities which have lost their competitive advantage become de-capitalised and de-manned as a natural consequence of other sectors' growing attractiveness. No amount of state subsidisation will restore their lost competitiveness. If there *were* a reasonable chance that new capital and new management could do the trick, one has to explain (i) why the money cannot be raised on the market and (ii) why, if the market refuses to play, the state should. The market failure hypothesis would be much more plausible if it did not provide sophisticated arguments for transferring large sums of money to its alleged victims.[9]

One test of the viability of restructuring schemes would be to see if private entrepreneurs from outside the industry are prepared to risk a substantial amount of their own funds in a restructuring plan. Usually, government finance is treated as a lever with which to extract private funds from a reluctant banker: the process, to be a useful acid test of the commercial viability of the scheme, should, however, be reversed. Government funds, if any, should only be made available to those schemes which are already funded privately and which are deemed particularly desirable in terms of non-economic objectives pursued by government.

There is a problem in most West European countries of capital-market imperfections: in particular, private venture capital has virtually disappeared and stock markets no longer function well enough to attract small investors. But to argue the case for subsidies on the grounds of capital-market imperfections is to compound the problem: two wrongs don't make a right. The best policy would be to try to improve the functioning of the private capital market.

Picking the Winners

The infant-industry argument has long been accepted as valid in theory. It allows a non-industrialised country to stimulate the creation of local industries, which are not immediately competitive with foreign producers, but which have a good chance of becoming so once firms have accumulated experience and progressed down the learning curve. In practice, it has proved difficult (although not impossible) to pick the right industries. Yet the task is comparatively easy in developing countries since all one has to do is survey existing industries in more advanced countries and select those which look fairly easy to develop back home.

The task is different if one is already an advanced country. One can, of course, look at what firms in the most advanced economy are doing and try to do the same (viz. the European space launcher project, which is no different from what developing countries try to do when they build up a motorcar industry). But one can also try to look beyond what is being done anywhere in the world. In neither instance, it is often argued, will the market come forward spontaneously, because entrepreneurs are too interested in short-term profits, reluctant to bear high risks, cannot divide up the required investment over time, and may be unable to 'appropriate' the results of their work if it turns out to be successful. In order to guarantee future progress, both for its own sake and relative to other countries, government stimulus is considered necessary.

To some extent most governments already encourage investments in high-risk ventures by sponsoring research activities, by offering special depreciation provisions for investment in research and development or by directly and indirectly subsidising innovations – and most people would agree that of all the things on which government could spend its tax-gotten gains, education, research, innovation and development surely rank very highly indeed.

General investment in education and scientific advance is obviously basic, but selective support for commercial research and development is much more problematic. Resources being limited, the state cannot and, indeed, should not support all projects indiscriminately. But 'picking the winners' is difficult (if it were not, we would all be. millionaire entrepreneurs). Over-generous subsidisation to support the creation of commercially useful technology might encourage firms to re-invent the wheel and earn great acclaim thereby.

Even if something new were to come of it, the question of the opportunity cost of creating new technology as opposed to that of adapting existing technology, or simply buying it, naturally arises. It is obviously cheaper in many cases to follow than to lead, unless one has a clear comparative advantage in a particular field. As in restructuring, the acid test of commercial viability should be applied to any selective government support for a high-risk and high-technology project; and this can be easily measured by the amount of private capital the venture succeeds in attracting. The government can then simply select those projects that fit in best with its non-economic objectives for special support. Even in non-commercial basic scientific research, there is a great deal to be said for avoiding international duplication of effort and specialising in one's area of comparative advantage.

Market 'Myopia'

To the extent that the market does look ahead – and the fact that privately funded research and development is still larger than public expenditure on research and development in most OECD countries suggests that it does – the objection is that it fails to predict society's future needs adequately. For example, heavy over-investment in man-made fibre capacity in the 1960s failed to take account either of the rise in the price of oil or of the change in tastes in favour of the natural fibres which took place in the early 1970s. But who could have predicted either of these occurrences? It is easy to be wise after the event. More generally, the market will fail to husband the earth's exhaustible resources for future generations, since the natural rationing mechanism of higher prices only comes into play when there is an actual shortage and not before.

All this is true – the market is by no means perfect – but can governments do better? Sometimes they can (Charles Kindleberger, the American economist, cites the building-up of the strategic materials stockpile in the United States, decided upon just before the outbreak of World War II, as being a smart move on the part of Herbert Feis[10]), but over time the likelihood of governments out-performing the market is not great, because they do not have access to superior information on society's future needs and scarcities.

Furthermore, if government takes it upon itself to attempt to guide the economy in a particular direction, it may discourage and finally extinguish private attempts to look forward into the future – an aspect of the 'crowding out' argument. Thus the choice may not be between having the market *and* the government working together to anticipate society's future needs or relying solely on the market, in which case government's role would be one of supporting market forces in a presumbably useful manner; instead, it may be between having more government and less market or less government and more market decisions. If the crowding-out hypothesis is correct, then even the best-intentioned government policies designed to supplement market forces will have nil, negligible or negative effects. Even if the crowding-out hypothesis is not correct, the cost of entrusting a more-than-marginal role in determining the future to government is, as mentioned above, dangerous for individual liberty. Indirect confirmation of the crowding-out hypothesis as applied to entrepreneurship can be found in theories of organisational behaviour or, more specifically, in Robert K. Merton's theory of bureaucratic disfunction.[11] It has consequently been observed that people either behave spontaneously in accordance with collective goals or can be constrained to do so. Unfortunately, however, each successive constraint reduces the spontaneous response until ultimately the individual learns to rely exclusively on external stimuli to channel his behaviour. There is no reason to believe that the entrepreneurial function is any different. The market's ability to work spontaneously is eroded every time a government takes decisions on its behalf.

Another argument against positive industrial policies is that they are a highly convenient smoke-screen. Governments will always claim that their industrial policies are 'positive', do not harm other countries' interests, do not distort competitive conditions at home, do not raise prices to consumers and are based on rational economic criteria. One would not expect them to do otherwise. Yet in practice they often end up, perhaps unintentionally, committing some, if not all, of the above economic crimes. Why?

Some Inherent Contradictions of Industrial Policy

There are several reasons. First, in spite of the claim that the government can look ahead of the market in drawing up brave and long-term 'industrial strategies', when it actually comes down to day-to-day action most state interventions of a micro-economic nature take the form of stop-gap emergency measures dictated by the pressure of events. An accumulation of *ad hoc* interventions does not add up to an 'industrial strategy' and may not even amount to an 'industrial policy'. Moreover, short-term measures are often in contradiction to long-term strategic objectives: job-preservation schemes, for instance, conflict with the improvement of productivity.

The reason for straying temporarily from the straight and narrow long-term path is overriding political considerations. Elected governments are worried, as are their voters, with the here and now, not with the future. In the long run, as Keynes remarked, we are all dead. This means that, contrary to what the proponents of industrial policy claim, direct state action in practice tends to be dictated by extremely short-run, often highly partial, considerations.

But in reality one cannot usefully distinguish between the long run and the short: yesterday's solutions become today's problems all too soon. In fact yesterday's long run is lived every day. Thus, as state planners plunge from one emergency to the next, they move steadily away from their stated long-term objectives. At one moment the gap between the idea and the reality becomes apparent, by which time one has a monumental industrial problem on one's hands. *The Economist* has put the point gracefully: 'Be grateful that the full apparatus of state intervention did not exist when the textile industry's woes began, or Lancashire today would probably be making cambric (or Nottingham making lace) for Londoners to hand-stitch into corsets'.[12] Another example of this process at work is the European Community's steel industry. For years it has been shielded, one way or another, from competition and has not been permitted by government and trade unions alike to adopt the latest technology and shut down inefficient plants. After several years of this ostrich-like policy there emerged in the late 1970s a problem of such huge dimensions that the prospective nationalisation of the major parts of Western Europe's steel industry seems to be the only avenue left open.[13]

As a result, the past failures of industrial policy, instead of provoking society to question the wisdom of applying such measures in the first place, leads to their intensification, either because the problem is judged to be too enormous to risk leaving it to solve itself or because it is genuinely believed that a bit more government intervention (rather than a lot less) might do the trick. The inherent dynamics of industrial policy are such that, once started, it can only expand.

This process is further helped by the fact that some of the beneficiaries of industrial policy are also in a position to help influence the political decision-making process. I refer to the undoubtedly hard-working, sincere, genuinely well-intentioned and usually competent civil servants entrusted with its administration. People tend to believe in their work and, if society entrusts one with large and growing responsibilities backed with the majesty of government, the feeling that one is doing great and useful work must be difficult to resist. The constituency in favour of expanding state intervention therefore tends to include not only its direct beneficiaries outside in the market place but large numbers of civil servants who genuinely believe that they are improving things. And their role in general policy formulation in modern government is widely considered to be substantial.[14] One can only salute and commend as exceptional the British Treasury's 'secret' paper in 1979 (duly leaked to the press), doubting the wisdom of the Government's spending another $1600 million on such worthy projects as the Rolls-Royce 535 engine, Airbus and a further consignment of subsidised ships to Poland.[15] Once more, the question is not so much whether and, if so, by how much economic efficiency is improved or impaired, but how large a state sector is compatible with the preservation of individual liberty.

Finally, the international repercussions of domestic industrial policies constitute an additional factor in the dynamics of expansion.

International Implications of Industrial Policy

Industrial policy has been increasingly substituted for traditional commercial policy in general and for tariff policy in particular. It therefore raises all the problems of international economic conflict and cooperation that have become so familiar in the GATT. Unlike tariffs, however, the international regulation of industrial policy is in its infancy and the danger of unintentional escalation is therefore considerable.

It is a favourite argument of theoretical economists that subsidies are preferable to tariffs as instruments of industrial policy. Tariffs are notoriously hard to measure and have numerous undesirable side effects. Outright subsidies to eligible industries are preferable because (i) they can be measured and (ii) they do not (as a tariff does) raise prices for consumers, reduce their real incomes and reduce demand. But this argument cannot be applied to industrial policy as it is practised in Western Europe. In answer to the arguments of economists, Edmund Dell remarked, shortly after resigning as Britain's Secretary of State for Trade, that 'a molehill of truth has resulted in a mountain of subsidies'.[16] Two arguments come to mind. First, industrial policies do not usually take the form of easy-to-measure outright subsidies, but of obscure non-tariff measures, the effects of which are harder to quantify than those of tariffs and much more elusive. Secondly, whereas tariffs are subject to a considerable amount of treaty law under the GATT and various regional trade organisations, industrial policy in general and subsidies in particular remain largely within the province of national sovereignty.[17]

In response to this legal vacuum, the principal trading members of the GATT devoted much effort during the six-year Tokyo Round negotiations to a 'subsidies and countervailing duties' code. In the meantime, the only constraint on governments in the application of their industrial policies was the threat that other countries might introduce offsetting duties on the products that had benefitted from government aid of one kind or another and that had been exported. The Code on Subsidies and Countervailing Measures is meant to clarify the conditions under which countries introduce such duties, especially with regard to the type of subsidies they are supposed to countervail. It constitutes a start, albeit a very small one (as discussed in Chapter 1), to bringing national industrial policies into the international arena. One serious drawback has been that the United States has been drawn into the system. Before the Trade Agreements Act of 1979, implementing the Tokyo Round agreements, the United States applied its own domestic trade law to other countries' subsidies and it was much stricter than any found in the GATT: it provided for the mandatory application of countervailing duties to any product bearing any subsidy, whether or not it caused damage to an American producer. In the GATT, as explained earlier, countervailing duties may only be applied against imports assisted by subsidies if they cause 'material' injury to local firms. Had it not been, then, for the deterrent effect of American law, the spread and growth of subsidisation might have been even greater than it anyway has been.

As it is, governments have used their legal freedom to introduce industrial policies at will. Such policies have spread like wildfire, partly through the international demonstration effect (the French system of indicative planning has been much admired and frequently – although not always successfully – imitated), partly in self-defence as governments attempt to offset the effects of other countries' industrial policies on their own economies by adopting similar ones and partly spontaneously. Even if a country has no wish to introduce industrial policies itself, and limits its offsetting action to countervailing duties (the United States being a case in point), other countries' industrial policies may harm its export interests in third countries. Firms may then ask for an offsetting export subsidy or equivalent support, as for instance International Telephones and Telecommunications (ITT) and General Electric (the American group) did in 1979 to help them secure large contracts in Egypt in competition with subsidised West European tenders.[18] Thus a reluctant government may be enticed indirectly into the system of competing industrial policies and one should not be surprised if one day it ends up with an 'industrial strategy' of its own.

Industrial policies are therefore catching; and, like escalating tariffs, they will gradually reduce trade governed by market forces to a minimum and ultimately cut the basis for income and productivity growth well below what otherwise would have been attainable.

Nor is this all. Industrial policy is not only a substitute for trade policy: it is also a complement. When used together with trade measures, especially orderly marketing arrangements, industrial policies create virtually insuperable barriers to trade. It is no accident that in areas troubled by strong import competition, like steel and textiles, there should be a conjunction of both informal trade restrictions and direct government support.[19] Such branches of industry are gradually being removed from the discipline of the market and increasingly resemble the agricultural sector. If one thinks of how agriculture has escaped the post-war trade liberalisation movement and how acrimonious have been international relations in this area,[20] the prospect of thereby enlarging the domain of non-market production and trade bodes ill for the future.

Rightful Role of the State: Public versus Private Goods

The state performs a vital and growing function in society. Increasingly urbanised and specialised societies require ever more extensive and sophisticated public goods. Cleaner towns, cleaner air and water ways, better education, better communications, better personal security and transport, more extensive collectivisation of risk, better cultural and recreational facilities. These are examples of modern goods and services which are increasingly provided by the state, either for social reasons or because of their intrinsic public goods' nature: namely, the quantity available does not diminish with enjoyment thereof (for example, cleaner air, public parks, security, justice) or it is costly and inconvenient to charge for them *pro rata* consumption (for example, bridges, drains, roads). Increasingly it is simply considered to be socially more acceptable to have a public rather than a private source of supply for certain services (notably health and education). These are 'private' goods in that there is no difficulty in dividing up the supply and making people pay individually for each unit they consume. They have a 'public' good element, however, in that to belong to a group of healthy and well-educated people is of benefit to each member.

But the provision by the state of private goods such as health, education, sewage *et cetera* has a paternalistic side to it. If the purpose is to make sure that all members of society, from the rich to the poor, have access to these 'essential' services, then the only non-distorting way of doing so is to redistribute income, and let private suppliers respond to the extra demand thus created. But there is always a lurking fear in the minds of the well-intentioned social engineers who develop welfare systems that the poor might not spend their income supplements on health and education, but on something less 'useful', like riotous living. In order to make sure that everybody consumes the 'right' amount of education and medical care, it is therefore safer to provide them free of charge at public expense and not give people an opportunity to choose (hence the element of paternalism). In this way the poor do not actually get the money obtained on their behalf from the rich, but get free services instead, which of course they would be foolish not to consume.

In fact, the private cost to consumers being zero, demand expands rapidly (and is, indeed, infinite if marginal utilities remain positive). In such circumstances the state has only two options: either allow demand to exceed supply and let queues form (for example, the National Health Service in Britain) or invest in extra capacity to meet the voracious demand (for example, state housing).

The first option gives rise to uncomplimentary remarks about the efficiency of the state and is often inequitable; the second solution costs a great deal of money and will, in due course, lead to over-investment in those particular sectors. This has two more negative implications: first, there is a built-in tendency for the state sector to expand at the expense of the private; and second, to the extent that governments tend to run into such awkward things as taxpayers' revolts and elections, there exists a tendency towards budget deficits and the inflationary financing thereof.

There is really no longer any reason, in Western Europe, in the latter part of the twentieth century, to continue treating lower-income groups as if they were retarded children. In the name of what principle should governments decide for individuals how they should spend the money collected by the state for the purpose of redistribution? Why cannot individuals be free to spend it as they wish? Certain limits on freedom of individuals might be desirable in view of the positive externalities of health and education, and it might be necessary to lay down a minimum consumption of both by law. Provision would have to be made for the chronically ill by raising their income supplements to offset their higher-than-average medical expenditures, but it would be quite possible to solve these problems while letting private demand and private supply of these services find a price which clears the market and which stops demand from reaching infinity. This would abolish queues and/or overcome the built-in tendencies towards the expansion of the public sector and chronic inflation.

According to Arthur Seldon, of the Institute of Economic Affairs in London,[21] the proportion of the British Government's expenditure which goes on true public goods (law and order, defence *et cetera*) amounts to only 15 per cent of the total budget, while that spent on essentially private goods (education, health, housing, sewage, transport) is a massive 40 per cent. Returning these to the private sector would reduce their cost to the nation

(a) because competition would make them more cost-conscious, and

(b) because demand would be rationed by price and society would not have to produce (at increasing marginal cost) the virtually worthless units (in terms of marginal utility) to satisfy excess demand at artificially low or even nil prices.

Such a reform, while not denying the rightful role of the state in providing true public goods, and possibly some semi-public goods, is becoming increasingly urgent, partly because Western Europe is no longer rich enough to be able to afford the luxury of massively misallocating its resources (is any country, for that matter?) and partly because ways must be found to reduce the trend rise in governments' share in GNP if the private sector is to survive at all.

Leaving the economic sphere, and entering, with temerity, the political domain, it is quite conceivable that West European governments have neglected law and order and especially defence, because they have been so preoccupied with the provision of private goods for welfare purposes. As Frank H. Knight, the American economist, once remarked 'liberty may be advocated, within wide limits, as an alternative to the government crippling itself for possible useful functions by attempting what it cannot perform'.[22] Thus the present weakness of Western Europe's military defences is another reason for restoring large chunks of modern government apparatus to the private sector.

NOTES

1. James E. Meade, *The Intelligent Radical's Guide to Economic Policy: the Mixed Economy* (London: Allen & Unwin, 1975) pp. 13 and 14.

2. *Ibid.*, p. 15.

3. D. L. Hodgson, 'Government Industrial Policy', *National Westminster Bank Quarterly Review*, London, August 1977, pp. 6–18.

4. S. C. Littlechild, *The Fallacy of the Mixed Economy* (London: Institute of Economic Affairs, 1978) p. 68.

5. Gerard and Victoria Curzon, *Hidden Barriers to International Trade*, Thames Essay No. 1 (London: Trade Policy Research Centre, 1970) p. 3.

6. N. Jequier, 'Computers', in Raymond Vernon (ed.), *Big Business and the State* (London: Macmillan, 1974) p. 219.

7. The open encouragement to the Japanese steel and textile industries to migrate to South Korea and Taiwan being a case in point.

8. There is broad agreement among economists that some 'socialisation of risk' is desirable, if only to defuse protectionist pressure and general resistance to change.

9. In Martin Wolf, *Adjustment Policies and Problems in Developed Countries*, Working Paper No. 349 (Washington: World Bank, 1979), there is advocated 'carefully designed general industrial, regional and manpower policies' to help firms, workers and regions affected by structural decline.

James Cassing advocates, in Irving Leveson and James W. Wheeler (eds), *Western Economies in Transition: Structural Change and*

Adjustment in Industrial Countries (Boulder: Westview Press, for the Hudson Institute, 1980), that assistance should only be afforded to workers and regions.

The present author's preference would be to use outright subsidies only for workers and use a spectrum of tax breaks for the conduct of regional policy. This would ensure that regional assistance would be positively related to market success, instead of being a hit-or-miss affair, as under the more ubiquitous *ex ante* regional investment grant system.

For a comparison of the different approaches of the main inter-governmental organisations to the problem of adjustment, as set out in their publications, see Wolf, 'Tower of Babel: Conflicting Ideologies of Adjustment', *The World Economy*, December 1979.

10. Charles P. Kindleberger, *Government and International Trade*, Essays in International Finance (Princeton: Princeton University, 1978) p. 13.

11. Robert K. Merton, 'The Unanticipated Consequences of Purposive Social Action', *American Sociological Review*, vol. I, 1936, pp. 894–904.

12. *The Economist*, 19 August 1978, p. 55.

13. For a discussion of the situation in the steel industry of the European Community, see Kent Jones, 'Forgetfulness of Things Past: the European Steel Cartel', *The World Economy*, May 1979.

14. In some countries enjoying representative government public attention has been focussing on how the power of the executive can be contained by the legislature. See, for example, Geoffrey Smith, *Westminster Reform: Learning from Congress*, Thames Essay No. 19 (London: Trade Policy Research Centre, 1979).

15. *Financial Times*, 1 March 1979, p. 18.

16. Edmund Dell, 'The Wistful Liberalism of Deepak Lal', *The World Economy*, May 1979, which was a reply to Deepak Lal, 'The Wistful Mercantilism of Mr Dell', *The World Economy*, June 1978.

17. See Gerard Curzon and Victoria Curzon Price, 'The Undermining of the World Trade Order', *Ordo*, May 1979, pp. 383–407. Although GATT rules with respect to subsidies and state enterprises are fairly comprehensive, and all signatory countries can seek redress under the 'nullification and impairment' clause, in practice these provisions are ignored by the guilty and not invoked by the injured.

18. *Financial Times*, 20 March 1979, p. 15.

19. In this connection, see Jan Tumlir, 'Salvation Through

Cartels? On the Revival of a Myth', *The World Economy*, October 1978.

20.   If one has any doubts on the matter, see the analysis by D. Gale Johnson, *World Agriculture in Disarray* (London: Macmillan, for the Trade Policy Research Centre, 1973).

21.   Arthur Seldon, 'Micro-economic Controls: Disciplining the State by Pricing', in *The Taming of Government* (London: Institute of Economic Affairs, 1979) pp. 67–84.

22.   Frank H. Knight, *Risk, Uncertainty and Profit* (Boston and New York: Houghton Mifflin, 1921).

CHAPTER THREE

Industrial Policy in Selected Community Countries

This chapter and the next will attempt to present in a factual manner the principal features of industrial policy in various countries of the European Community and those being pursued at Community level. It will permit the discussion to move from the abstract issues discussed in Chapter 2 to practical problems of public policy.

France: le Plan

The discussion shall start with France because there the state has a long tradition of deep involvement in the economy which has served as a model for others. Successive British governments have looked wistfully over the Channel at the seeming ease with which 'le Plan' launched France on a high growth path and brought her industry up to world competitive standards. The Federal Republic of Germany, too, was intrigued enough by French 'indicative planning' to adopt something very similar, although German traditions were probably uppermost in this development. Smaller West European countries have not had to create elaborate structures to develop close links between industry and the state – it was all in the family anyhow – but they also have not been indifferent to the French example.

The single most important feature is, obviously, 'le Plan'. It is significant not because it really 'plans' the French economy. It does not. It is significant because it creates close links between industry and the state. Indeed, the relationship is close enough to merit the description of 'partnership'. Charles-Albert Michalet puts it this way:

The Commissions du Plan have contributed largely toward bringing together the state on the one hand and large enterprises on the other. The Commissariat du Plan has played a technical role at the heart of the negotiation, which [Andrew] Shonfield has not hesitated to classify as a 'conspiracy': a conspiracy between high functionaries and directors of enterprises who speak the same language, have a similar education, belong to the same social milieu and often are destined eventually to find themselves side by side in the same administration councils.[1]

In fact, the French Government has perhaps the best information-gathering system of any large West European country. The 'Plan' is in fact largely an information-gathering exercise conducted by industry and the state and its targets are the outcome of the data thus acquired (they are not imposed upon private industry in a Soviet-style straightjacket). It is noteworthy that 'representatives of the workers' unions and of the consumers, have played only a minor role' in the information gathering.[2] Another information-gathering system is provided by three decades of strict price control which the present French Government is in the process of abolishing.

Besides 'le Plan', the French state is anyway extensively involved in such sectors as insurance, telecommunications, electronics, gas, coal, oil refining, transport, steel, chemicals, motor cars, aviation, computers and nuclear energy. According to one source, however, although operations of state-owned companies are often integrated into the Government's overall economic planning, they are generally regarded as managed on sound business principles, by contrast to their counterparts in the United Kingdom, Sweden and Italy. They are rarely accused of gross inefficiency or of maintaining employment at the expense of profits.[3]

In late 1977 it was announced that state enterprises would be offered a formal contract between themselves and the state, drawing a careful line between their commercial and political responsibilities. The latter would be costed and the state would provide the appropriate compensation amount in the form of a grant. This scheme, for instance, will compensate Air France for flying *Concorde*, or Charbonnages de France for keeping open non-economic mines, and it will permit their managements to turn in respectable commercial results for the remainder. This is an excellent solution to the problem of measuring the economic performance of the state and the value of its non-economic objectives and has attracted considerable comment in the United Kingdom.

In addition to this extensive state participation in the economy, the French Government has the ultimate instrument of control over industry in its hands: the banking sector and the government can reward or punish firms with ease by offering or withholding credit.

Paradoxically, in spite of this highly sophisticated state-industry structure, French industrial policy has not got out of control. On the contrary, the Government has taken a hard line against the featherbedding of industry. It has provided its own internal control. In more profligate hands, though, the system could be distinctly inflationary and in fact in the few months before the March 1978 elections many failing enterprises were kept alive on lengthening credit lines. After the defeat of the Socialist–Communist coalition, the Government coolly allowed those enterprises to go under.

In 1974, in the wake of the 'Plan de Refroidissement Fourçade', the French Government established a body to coordinate all distress signals emanating from the economy and being received by various ministries which, one way or another, had a bearing on French industry. The 'Comité interministériel pour l'aménagement des structures industrielles' (CIASI) is an extremely high-level group of ministers and top civil servants whose job is to find cures for sick firms.[4] The CIASI meets once a week and has treated some 500 'patients', among them such well-known firms as Citroen, Boussac, Poclain, Manufrance and Schlumpf. The CIASI has discovered that a frequent cause of firms' difficulties is simply poor management, which the recession since 1974 has laid bare, rather than the recession itself. Poor recruiting policies, bad personnel management, primitive accounting controls ('*Ils ne connaissent pas leur prix de revient, alors ils percutent le plantane sans s'en rendre compte*'[5]) and, finally, lethal mistakes in past investment decision are all cited as affecting at least two out of three of the CIASI's patients.

The cures, not all of which work, as the failure of the 1975 'Plan Boussac' testifies, comprise surprisingly little hard cash. The CIASI's universal remedy is to select a healthy firm in the same line of business and persuade it to take over its ailing competitor. This was, for instance, used with gratifying success when loss-making Citroen was taken over by Peugeot in 1975. The unwilling groom in these shot-gun weddings is duly rewarded with a suitable dowry, in the form of loans or bank credits, with a veritable drop of outright state grants or subsidised loans from the 'Fonds de Développement Economique et Social' (FDES). As a CIASI official is reported to have said: '*Nous sommes le soupçon qui fait prendre la mayonnaise.*'[6] The CIASI has been criticised for this policy, because from time to time a healthy firm, instead of curing the ailing one, catches the disease itself – which makes two problems out of one. Peugot-Citroen, for instance, is clearly suffering from severe indigestion after having absorbed Talbot-Simca-Chrysler in 1980.

Another method, if a suitable bridegroom cannot be found, is to evict the existing management, write down assets and shut down the least efficient productive units. This industrial surgery, painful though it is, has recently acquired strong advocates in the higher echelons of the French Government. The Paris Correspondent of the *Financial Times* has cited André Giraud, as Minister of Industry, as saying:

> You cannot ask the state to guarantee the present number of jobs in every one of France's 42 000 enterprises.[7]

He has also cited René Monory, as Minister of Economic Affairs, as saying:

> The more you assist the economy, the more you destroy progressive imagination, pugnacity and creativity and the less competitive you ultimately become.[8]

Finally Raymond Barre, as Prime Minister, has been cited in *L'Expansion* as saying:

> We must not hesitate to cut out the dead wood; that is, the sectors where we cannot compete. The future of France does not depend on the number of ships which we build at a loss, nor on the production of steel which we cannot sell.[9]

Mr Barre continued with a precise statement:

> The role of the state is to say to the 'patrons': So you want to do such and such? We'll help you. But if in five years you have not succeeded, we'll drop you. There must be a [market] sanction.[10]

This unheard of respect for market forces did not mean that the French Government was about to make a 180-degree turn and start dismantling its well-developed structures for active and reactive industrial policy. But it did suggest that its formidable apparatus was likely to be pointed in a new direction – that of promoting rather than resisting industrial change.

The Government's uncompromising attitude to the collapse of the Boussac textile empire in 1978 and to the bankruptcy in the same year of Terrin, France's largest ship-repairer, is significant. It braved the inevitable trade union response: a strike at Terrin by the Communist-led Confederation General du Travail (CGT) and a major CGT-offensive at Renault, the state-owned motor-car producer and traditionally the weak spot in the governmental defences. For the first time since World War II, Renault stood firm, decided on a lockout, moved machines from one site to another to maintain production, dismissed over 50 workers and refused to negotiate until the others had returned to work.

The Government's attitude to receivership is also significant: 'There's nothing disastrous about receivership: it enables the company to function and customer uncertainty to be lifted'.[11] An economist can only applaud this correct but largely misunderstood function of bankruptcy in a market-economy system: bankruptcy does not destroy physical assets, but it devalues them and gives a new management team a chance to make a proper return on investment or allows more efficient firms to expand by taking up the space left by the bankrupt firm. The French system of carefully scrutinising ailing firms before they 'go bust' may help to ensure that precious non-physical assets, such as unique research teams, are not lost in the restructuring process.

Further signs of a shift in emphasis toward greater reliance on private (as opposed to public) investment and market forces generally, are the abolition of price controls after three decades, effective as from September 1978 onwards,[12] and a reform in the tax laws which makes it possible for Frenchmen to deduct 5000 francs a year from their taxable income to invest in company shares.[13] It has been reported that this scheme has increased the number of people investing on the French stock market by 30 per cent in a year (1978) and may have contributed to the 45 per cent increase in French stock values recorded in 1978.[14] Further tax advantages are planned to promote investment in small firms.

The counterpart of the French Government's hard line with regard to uncompetitive firms and industries has been a growing number of special schemes to promote new investments in the areas most affected by redundancies: the money which is not spent on keeping declining sectors alive artificially is available to promote new investment in high-growth sectors – at least that is the theory.

The French Government, like all other governments in Western Europe, also offers incentives to invest in depressed regions, through the FDES, while the Institut pour le Développement Industriel (IDI) provides long-term finance on both a loan and equity basis to weak sectors. IDI, however, may only acquire shares in a private company on a temporary basis; it must try to sell them back to the public as soon as possible. There is also a state-run scheme for accelerating investment projects which would otherwise have been postponed and a Fonds d'Action Conjoncturelle which has one billion francs to spend on infrastructure projects in areas of high unemployment. A large sum (4330 million francs) was set aside in May 1978 to provide relief from social insurance contributions to employers of young people and to finance labour re-training schemes.

In addition, a Fonds Spécial d'Adaptation Industrielle (FSAI) was formed in September 1978, when the extent of the steel crisis became apparent. Any company may apply for a grant if it creates more than 50 jobs. Grants take the form of outright subsidies (amounting to 20 per cent of the cost of a new investment) or of soft loans bearing a fixed interest of 3 to 5 per cent, the actual rate depending on the financial success, or lack thereof, of the venture. The sums available for 1978–79 amounted to 3000 million francs. A state-supported export credit system has been estimated to cost the taxpayer about 10 per cent of every large contract.[15] Really giant structural problems, like coal, steel and shipbuilding, which in France as elsewhere carry heavy political risks, are shouldered by the President and his Prime Minister in person – with the help (or the hindrance) of the European Community. These are discussed in Chapter 4.

France therefore presents a paradoxical picture. On the one hand, she has a long tradition of direct and indirect state involvement in economic affairs and she has numerous public bodies through which industrial policy is exercised. On the other hand, since the elections in March 1978, there has been a clear attempt to try a new more market-oriented tack. How deep this change is cannot be gauged for the moment. The Government took steps to nationalise in part the French steel industry in the autumn of 1978 and it will clearly take more than a few declarations to reverse the deeply embedded tradition of state involvement. It is certainly not prepared to leave things to chance and is spending huge sums on attracting new industry to stricken regions: a prime example of a hybrid adjustment policy, the success of which cannot possibly be gauged for some years to come.

Germany: Emphasis on Concertation

The Federal Republic of Germany has a long history of state intervention in industrial development, dating back to Bismarck's tariff protection of the nascent coal-based steel industry in the 1880s, continuing through to the inter-war period. German economic thought also tended in this direction: while the British intellectual establishment was debating the ideas of Adam Smith, David Ricardo and John Stuart Mill, German thinkers discussed Friedrich List and Karl Marx.

Paradoxically, but understandably, after World War II the new Bundesrepublik turned its back on the experience of generations and embraced the liberal credo with enthusiasm, as much for political reasons (the guarantees of individual liberty and the small role reserved for the state) as for economic ones. The process of conversion is described by Adrian Crawley, in his book, *The Rise of Western Germany 1945–72*, in these terms:

> In a country where most people were still hungry, living in ruins and often in rags, the continuation of some form of rationing to ensure 'fair shares' seemed inevitable . . . [Ludwig] Erhardt [as Minister of Economics] took a different view. If individuals were given the chance, he believed, they would relieve the general want far more quickly than any state-controlled apparatus, however well intended. Where almost everything was lacking, there was unlimited opportunity for enterprise of every conceivable kind.[16]

Erhardt's policies worked like magic. In 1947 the Federal Republic's exports covered less than 40 per cent of its imports. By 1952 its balance of trade was in equilibrium and by 1954 its reserves of gold and dollars amounted to 11 000 million marks.

A large state-owned sector was inherited from the past. But it was run on strictly commerical lines and was in part sold off to the public. The private industrial sector revived with surprisingly little state intervention apart from initial subsidies financed by American aid.[17]

As the late Andrew Shonfield, the British journalist, pointed out in his book, *Modern Capitalism*,

> when the Germans began to reconstruct their economy, they built upon the familiar structural foundation and plan, much of it invisible to the naked eye, as if guided by an archaeologist who could pick his way blindfold about some favourite ruin.[18]

Large firms, once more, came to dominate key sectors such as oil and gas (with a four-firm concentration-ratio of 83.7 per cent in 1960), automobiles (81.3 per cent), shipbuilding (54.2 per cent), electric power (49.5 per cent), chemicals (49 per cent), electrical engineering (47.4 per cent), rubber and asbestos (45 per cent).[19]

The stage was therefore set for a subtle change in the relationship between industry and the state. In 1966 the Stability and Growth Act was promulgated, placing on the shoulders of the Federal Government the duty to achieve price-stability, economic growth and full employment, partly through macro-economic Keynesian policies to offset fluctuations in the business cycle and partly through concerted action on the part of federal, state and local authorities, labour unions and employers' associations. Just as indicative planning in France is liable to be misunderstood, because it does not involve planning *per se*, so concerted action in Germany is liable to be misunderstood because it does not involve action *per se*; rather it involves an effort, informal since the breakdown in 1977 of formal procedures, to concert *expectations* among different interests.

Thus, after a brief flirtation with classical liberalism (to which school a close business-government relationship is anathema), Germany reverted to a 'concerted economy' system. In doing so, she not only remained true to her own traditions, but also to those of mainland Western Europe in general. The 'concerted economy' embodied in law via the 1966 Stability and Growth Act resembled the French 'Plan' like a brother. Strangely, however, some romantic attachment to classical liberalism remains and much emphasis continues to be placed in West Germany on the virtues of free competition, market forces and entrepreneurship. (In this sense the German and French attitudes, having started from very different points after World War II, appear to have converged rather neatly.)

The concerted action process has been thus described by Georg Küster:

The strong sense of exclusivity in the concerted action process was intensified by its secrecy. No official list of regular participants existed and no detailed account of actual proceedings was made public . . . This attitude was explained by pointing to the advantages of secret negotiations, which were said to permit frank statements of views, and positions free of narrow sectarian interests . . . Indeed, elitist cooperation between government authorities and organised groups in the concerted action program had developed into a quasi-parliament for economic policy. Its participants discussed not only guidelines for income policy, but also matters of competition policy, trade policy and wealth policy.[20]

Professor Küster is clearly distressed by this development. But hindsight now permits us to say that the French system of close concertation between the state and industry is the norm rather than the exception in Western Europe. The essential difference is that in France trade unions are not (yet) involved in the interface between industry and the state, whereas in Germany they are (or were until 1977). The new British system also includes both sides of industry in permanent negotiations with the state.

Having established the 'listening posts' necessary for drawing up an effective government industrial policy, Germany proceeded to enact in 1969 legislation to improve the economic structure of lagging regions. Regional aid was provided in the form of investment subsidies, ranging from 15 to 25 per cent of the investment, depending on classification of the region on a scale which measured income, unemployment and lack of infrastructure. In 1975 a 'new approach' to regional problems was introduced, which involved *anticipating* (by means of forecasts) the socio-economic problems which could arise in the future, and taking the necessary steps to correct them in time. James Meade's 'intelligent radical' would be delighted by such foresight. It is, in fact, a tribute to the German concerted action system that the Government *in 1975*, after the oil crisis of 1973–74, felt sufficiently confident in its handling of current problems that it could enjoy the luxury of worrying about future ones. Sectoral aids were granted to shipbuilding to permit its survival in the face of competition from subsidised yards elsewhere, while coal-mining has for years been subsidised to help it compete with cheap oil imports, but on the whole the 'concerted economy' was averse to propping up unprofitable enterprises for their own sake. Positive help was provided also for certain key sectors, such as gas and petroleum, electronic components, aerospace, nuclear energy and tele-communications.

The Government actively encouraged mergers between German firms throughout the 1960s on the grounds that only large industrial units could hope to compete with American-based multinational enterprises. In 1973, under the Social Democrats, this policy went into reverse, as the authorities decided that excessive concentration might prove dangerous to competition. The cartel law was extended to cover *ex ante* control of mergers involving firms with a joint turnover of more than 250 million marks. Provision is made in the law for 'rescue mergers' and Karstadt, a major department store and travel agency, availed itself of this in November 1976 when it took over the large but bankrupt mail-order firm of Neckermann. Permission was only granted, however, because the two firms were in related but not competing sectors and if Neckermann disappeared there would only be two mail-order firms left in Germany.[21]

In fact, 'rescue mergers' are by no means a foregone conclusion. In 1975, the Federal Cartel Office refused to allow Thyssen Industrie AG to acquire Karl Huller GmbH, a bankrupt manufacturer of automated machine tools. Its argument was significant: Huller's market share of 25 per cent would be picked up anyway by the other firms in the sector and the largest part would go to the most efficient. The jobs lost by letting Huller disappear would reappear in the more efficient firms which would expand to meet the extra demand.[22] Where else in Western Europe could one find public expression of such serene confidence in the ability of the market to re-create lost jobs? It might be argued that the number of jobs lost in Huller was insignificant compared with those involved in the Neckermann failure, but the German Government does not fear large numbers of redundancies, as the Volkswagen case demonstrates.

In 1974, when Volkswagen made a loss of $300 million, the management decided that the necessary restructuring would involve 25 000 redundancies. The unions, not unnaturally, did not sanction the plan and the question of federal aid arose at one moment. But Hans Appel, as Minister of Finance, replied promptly: 'One federal railway and one agricultural policy are quite enough for me.'[23] The Federal Government *did* provide help, but not to Volkswagen directly: 250 million marks were set aside to encourage the creation of new activities in the regions affected by the redundancies and the company itself financed the necessary 'golden handshakes'. By the end of 1975, Volkswagen was once more making a profit and had taken on 4000 extra people.[24] The relocation of 25 000 Volkswagen workers cost the state only 8400 marks per worker. The case disproves the thesis that adjustment costs are lower if they are spread out over a long period of time. In fact, the opposite is true: costs are reduced to a bare minimum if the adjustment is made quickly. The labour relocation problem is also reduced, because a healthy and expanding firm becomes a source of new job opportunities.

The attitude of the German authorities to public subsidies for private industry, except in well-defined situations, is aptly illustrated by the following detail: A very small amount of direct aid was reported to have been provided to Volkswagen under the direct responsibility of Helmut Schmidt, as Chancellor, but this gave rise to court action on the grounds that it was unconstitutional! The contrast with the British Government's handling of British Leyland is striking.

There is no doubt that firms in difficulty in Germany are allowed to collapse. This exceptional self-restraint on the part of the Federal Government seems to be due to three main factors.

First, the Federal Government is committed to fighting inflation and, with an already heavy budget for social expenditure, could not take on a large public subsidisation programme without starting a new inflationary spiral.

Secondly, the unions are prepared to cooperate with industry and the state, in spite of growing levels of unemployment. This tripartite concertation process worked smoothly until 1977, when the long-standing mutual trust between employers and trade unions broke down. The employers' federation, the Bundesverband der Deutschen Industrie (BDA), brought a suit against the 'co-determination' law, providing for worker participation in the conduct of corporate affairs, due to enter into force on 1 July 1978, on the grounds that it interfered with the right of shareholders to dispose of their own property. In retaliation, the German trade union movement, the Deutscher Gewerkschaftbund (DGB), withdrew from the concerted action procedures,[25] with the result that 1978 saw some unusually bitter strikes, notably in the printing and engineering sectors. The annual DGB congress, held in May 1978, held out little hope for an improvement in relations with industry: it voted in favour of a 35-hour working week, the nationalisation of key industries (including banks and insurance companies) and for continuing the boycott of the concertation procedures.[26]

After the Federal Court handed down its decision on the 'co-determination'[27] issue in favour of the trade unions, and the economy was once more expanding, the unions reverted to their policy of constructive cooperation in the concertation process.

Thirdly, Germany's unique relationship between banks and business has stood her in good stead during the recession. It is well known that Germany's 'universal' banking system ties the banks closely to industry by permitting them to hold shares in companies, and to appoint bank officials to firms' supervisory boards. Both these factors permit banks to have exceptionally detailed information about their customers (especially regarding their credit-worthiness) and they are not shy of stepping in to protect their interests if they find that a firm is losing money. It has been said, for instance, that if 'British banks had been governed by similar rules, Rolls-Royce would not have been allowed to collapse. Moreover . . . AEG–Telefunken, rescued in 1975 by the Dresdner Bank in particular and the country's universal banking system in general, would probably have gone to the wall if it had been a British company'.[28] Subsequent events cast some doubt on the wisdom of having rescued AEG–Telefunken: in spite of a bank-sponsored restructuring plan and a change of management, the firm continued to lose money at the rate of several million marks a year, culminating in a loss of almost one billion marks in 1979 alone. A new effort to restructure the company was announced in December 1979, suggesting that banks, no less than governments, dislike admitting defeat.[29]

In theory, Germany's 'universal' private banks spot trouble before it gets out of hand and take the type of action that in France is undertaken – often too late – by the CIASI; namely, the rationalisation of production, the shutting down of inefficient plants, and the finding of suitable bridegrooms for companies in distress. As one West German banker put it: 'It is very important to know, that it is possible to step in and sort out a mess if it is necessary. Naturally, one still has a responsibility to one's depositors; that is unchanged . . . '.[30] In practice, the example of AEG–Telefunken shows how far a powerful banking system can go in resisting the verdict of the market and ignoring the best interests of its depositors and shareholders.

While on the subject of banking, it is interesting to note that in France the nationalised banking sector has been criticised for having allowed firms to borrow short-term in 1972–73 to finance investments which turned sour in 1975–77[31] (the acid-test of commercial viability being absent in both cases, making it impossible to draw neat distinctions as to how differently state and private banks behave).

Thus German industrial policy combines a maximum of *concertation between* employers, employees and the state, with a minimum of actual *intervention by* the state. The hand of the state is seen discreetly from time to time, in regional aid policy, in subsidising coal production, in promoting certain high-technology sectors and in occasionally providing adjustment assistance as in the case of Volkswagen. In the case of company failures, the state will not provide assistance, although the private banking system may do so. The key element in German industrial policy is anti-trust legislation, which seeks to encourage competition to a degree that is unique in Western Europe. German industrial policy differs from French in this crucial respect. The 'concerted action' system in Germany seems, paradoxically, to be compatible with the preservation of competition – a unique squaring of the circle. This may be due to the fact that the principal purpose of the concerted-action system is not to plan the economy, or to channel it into a given direction, but to reach a consensus between employers and employees on the semi-permanent restructuring process. It is also helped by the open nature of the German economy.

There are many features in both the French and German approaches to industrial policy which are compatible with the preservation or enhancement of the market's role in factor allocation. The next three countries discussed – Britain, Italy and the Netherlands – offer, on the other hand, practical instances of some of the drawbacks outlined in Chapter 2.

United Kingdom: Indecision[32]

British industrial policy has its roots in the Great Depression when the 1934 Regional Industries Act was passed to promote industrial development in the hardest-hit industries, namely shipbuilding, steel, coal and heavy engineering. *Plus ça change* . . .

Unlike the French, however, the British Government considered industrial policy essentially in terms of solving regional problems rather than in terms of national industry as such. One of the principal instruments of British industrial policy was, and indeed still is, the Industrial Development Certificate, introduced in 1945, which directed new investment (especially foreign) towards areas of above-average unemployment. The logic behind this policy was that, as Adam Smith remarked, 'a man is of all sorts of luggage the most difficult to be transported' and it seemed common sense to bring the job to the worker, rather than the worker to the job. It is not as simple as that and an *a priori* case could be made attributing part of the reason for Britain's industrial decline to the systematic redeployment of new investment to peripheral regions. In 1964 Regional Development grants were introduced at a rate of 40 per cent of investment costs in assisted areas. But it was only in 1972, after the emergency rescue of Rolls-Royce by the Conservative Government of Edward Heath (committed to the old-fashioned free-market virtues of competition) that a more integral view of industrial policy began to emerge. The Industry Act 1972 gave the government discretionary powers (which the French had had for a long time) to help any industry in distress irrespective of its geographical location. In 1974 the Labour Government of Harold Wilson went a step further by introducing '*planning agreements*' to be concluded individually between the government and major firms in key industrial sectors. These were the intellectual successors of Britain's first attempt at 'indicative planning' (undertaken in 1961 after an ill-fated attempt to copy the French system). The idea now, as it was then, is to achieve a better coordination of markets by attempting to forecast and match up input and output requirements. Firms, it was argued, could produce more efficiently, foresee bottlenecks and identify future gluts if all market participants pooled their information on proposed investment, prices, market growth, international competition and technological change. What was overlooked in 1961 was the need to introduce flexibility into planning agreements to accommodate market change. Now planning agreements are flexible – but then, asks S. C. Littlechild in the essay cited earlier, what is their use? If they adapt to market change, one might as well do without.[33]

The answer to this pertinent question may well have been given by Ronald Grierson, a director of the General Electric Company (the British firm) and a former Director-General for Industrial Policy in the Commission of the European Community: Corporatism is a frame of mind in which producers, instead of facing the risks and penalties and, of course, also the rewards of the free market, huddle together in the bunkers of Whitehall and Millbank and, in the name of some mystical public interest, try to rationalise their relationship with each other and with the government of the day.[34] Mr Grierson's point is an important one: the chief executives of large public corporations, after an initial conditioned reflex – perhaps! – of shying away from so close a link with government officials and their principal competitors, can usually be relied upon to support the system. It, after all, introduces an element of stability and certainty in a very changeable world. Did not Sir John Hicks remark that the best form of monopoly profit is a quiet life? From such motives springs a large and growing constituency in favour of 'indicative planning' from within the private industrial sector itself.

Apart from planning agreements, which concern only the largest firms, the United Kingdom's National Economic Development Council, affectionately known as Neddy, centralises information for the rest of industry. It is composed of representatives from both sides of industry as well as government officials. It has given birth to a host of 'little Neddies' – 39 at the last count – each concerned with gathering and coordinating information on as many 'key sectors' of British industry. Thus, for the first time, Britain has a structured information-gathering system. There is, however, little evidence that there is any inter-ministerial coordination, as in France. Indeed, the Department of Industry and the Department of Trade were split in 1974 and, it is said, tread different and often crossed paths, besides waging sporadic war on the Treasury.

It is early yet to judge whether the 'Thirty Nine Steps' will work. By involving worker representatives in the planning process, the Government may succeed in convincing the trade unions that they have to become more flexible, permit retraining and allow redundancies in order for British industry to remain competitive at high rates of pay. If so, this will be an invaluable achievement. On the other hand, if it fails (and there is no reason for optimism) all that will have been achieved is a reduction of competition and increased reliance on the process of huddling together in the bunkers of Whitehall and Millbank.

Another element in British industrial policy structure is the National Enterprise Board (NEB), launched in 1975, by the radical

Minister of Industry, Anthony Wedgwood Benn. The NEB was given an initial capital fund of £700 million (at the time worth $1400 million) with which it was supposed to acquire a share in the *profitable* end of British industry. Why, the question was asked, should the state always be left with all the lame ducks? But the NEB's 'guidelines' state: 'There may also be other occasions when the NEB are directed by the Secretary of State under Section 3 of the Industry Act 1975 to provide assistance to companies in difficulty, and in these cases there may not be a normal return for some time'.[35] What a monument of understatement!

In fact, the NEB was given two difficult, and in practice, incompatible tasks:

(a) the promotion . . . of industrial efficiency and international competitiveness
and,
(b) the provision, maintenance or safeguarding . . . of employment.[36]

Most economists would maintain that objective 'b' follows naturally from objective 'a', providing industrial efficiency and productivity are genuinely pursued, even at the cost of raising unemployment during an initial period of adaptation. Any attempt, though, to put 'b' before 'a' will, like the proverbial cart and horse situation, bring the dynamic process of change to a halt.

In the event, the NEB was created just in time to fly to the help of British Leyland, the huge motor vehicle manufacturer, Alfred Herbert, manufacturer of machine tools, and a series of small and exceedingly sick companies. It also took over the Government's shares in Rolls-Royce, quite clearly having decided to pursue objective 'b' at the expense of objective 'a'.

Even as a provider of state equity finance to viable commercial businesses, the NEB is fraught with contradiction. If a firm has good prospects but needs equity, this can usually be found (if it cannot, one must ask why not). In Britain, although the private venture capitalist is largely extinct, killed off by a punitive tax system, the institutional venture capitalist exists under the guise of such bodies as Equity Capital for Industry Ltd, or the Industrial and Commercial Financial Corporation.[37] If a promising firm is turned down by any of the these sources of venture capital, it can indeed turn to the NEB for finance, but this means that, by definition, the NEB must make-do with the private sector's left-overs. It is doomed to acquire more than its fair share of duds. The NEB can, indeed, fill a gap in the market by providing high-risk finance to firms with longish odds against success, but which could pay off handsomely in the future (Rolls-Royce perhaps). On the other hand, they could just as well flop. The question is *how much* risk the Government should shoulder at taxpayers' expense, because if the market refuses to take certain risks, they may not be worth taking.

The question arose again with the NEB's decision to enter the semi-conductor business[38] possibly a sensible decision in itself, but one which has been greeted with sour scepticism because it was taken by an institution whose reputation for sound business management has been tarnished by such resounding disasters as British Leyland and Alfred Herbert.

Besides the National Enterprise Board, which supplies state *equity* finance to promising or sinking firms, the Secretary of State for Industry may, under the provision of Section 8 of the 1975 Industry Act, help *any* firm *anywhere* in the United Kingdom with loans or grants. Schemes for helping firms are divided into three categories.[39]

There are *general* schemes of which the most representative is one to accelerate investments which would otherwise have been put off and which will – it is hoped – relieve potential capacity shortages identified in the little-Neddy working parties referred to above.

Secondly, there are some fifteen sectoral schemes in operation which have been devised on the basis of reports of little Neddies and which aim at a genuine restructuring of industry. They involve grants for the 4 Rs – re-equipment, rebuilding, rationalisation and restructuring.[40] This includes the scrapping of marginal capacity, but firms must undertake to try to find alternative employment for redundant workers within the industry.

Finally, there are 'individual applications' whereby firms may apply for aid outside the general or sectoral schemes. It is here that are found grants and loans for British Leyland and Chrysler.

In addition to general assistance throughout the United Kingdom, Section 7 of the 1972 Industry Act provides for selective assistance in 'assisted areas'. An Industrial Development Advisory Board (IDAB), consisting of eleven distinguished people drawn from industry, banking, management consultancy, labour, accountancy and academia, scrutinises all requests for government assistance under both Sections 7 and 8 of the 1972 Industry Act. Like the CIASI in France it attempts 'to preserve viable parts of the business, and the associated jobs, not by assisting the failed company itself, but by providing an incentive for a sound company to acquire the business as a going concern'.[41]

There seem to have been relatively few such shotgun weddings, however, and firms like British Leyland and Alfred Herbert are permitted to retain their independence – perhaps because no willing bridegroom can be found! Sometimes a foreigner is permitted to make off with the unwanted prize: the Roots Motor Company was acquired by Chrysler which in turn sold its British assets to Peugeot–Citroën in 1978, after the British Government had successfully resisted union pressure to merge them with British Leyland, and the company is now called Talbot.

British industrial policy would be incomplete without reference to the nationalised steel and shipbuilding industries, which have clocked up notoriously large losses in past years, but they will be discussed in the next chapter. One should also mention the temporary employment subsidy (discussed in greater detail below).

One possible effect of the accumulation of all these schemes to regenerate British industry is captured by an item, headed 'Last Resort', published in the diary column of the *Financial Times* on 27 June 1978:

Although for obvious reasons the names of the people involved cannot be revealed, this story I have garnered in Whitehall is entirely true. A company in a development area 'somewhere in England' had been given so many loans that the Department of Trade finally decided to call a halt. An official was sent up to convey this grim decision to the managing director.

A short while ago the official chanced to meet the managing director in the street and was invited by the latter to his flat for a drink. The flat proved to be most luxurious. The official apologised for having once been a bearer of painful news. 'Don't think about it, old boy,' said his host. 'There was no alternative, really. Things had got so bad for the company that I was almost being driven to using some of my own money!'

Observer

In other words, the acid test of some private capital participation in publicly-supported ventures, as a guarantee of commercial viability, does not seem always to be made. This leads one to the question of the control mechanisms in the structure of British industrial policy. In Britain, more than in France or Italy, Parliament keeps a fairly watchful eye on how public pennies are spent. If the government of the day, however, commands a majority of one in the House of Commons, its policies, after a show of debate, will be endorsed. Thus in May 1978, the Government was obliged to ask Parliament for an increase of £1500 million (up to £5500 million) in the British Steel Corporation's borrowing limits. In spite of vigorous Opposition criticism of the Government's handling of BSC's restructuring process, the Government won by 49 votes.[42]

Members of Parliament are increasingly anxious, though, to exercise full control over public funds once they have been voted. It was reported[43] that the Public Accounts Committee, in the House of Commons, had asked (unsuccessfully) to have an Auditor-General's Examination of the NEB's books, because it was not directly accountable to Parliament. This Committee later came up with proposals for far stricter audits of public aids as well as for a 'management audit' to determine the efficiency with which public funds are used. As a result, the Government now sets a 'required rate of return' of 5 per cent on all public investment in industry – a welcome departure from 'the nudge and fudge methods of the past'.[44]

If state-owned firms were to be made directly accountable to Parliament, an informed public debate would develop, on the basis of which Members of Parliament and their constituents would acquire a feeling for the trade-offs involved. Decisions involving large transfers of public funds to small sections of the population would have to be justified in terms of all the other interests represented in Parliament. At present Parliament exercises no effective control and is placed before a *fait accompli*.

Whilst direct parliamentary control at a micro-level may still be a long way off, the propping up of inefficient industry for employment reasons is no longer a sure road to re-election. The tax-paying public has begun to understand the trade-offs and it is highly significant that 'unpalatable but necessary decisions' to close old and inefficient steel-works have indeed been made[45] in spite of muted opposition from the trade unions. The main difference as compared with France, however, is that these decisions to make large numbers of workers redundant in the interests of efficiency have been forced upon an unwilling government by the shortage of resources and a belated and half-hearted decision to fight inflation, whereas in France they have been initiated by a convinced government. The effect in both countries depends to a very great extent on the reaction of the trade unions. The British system attempts to co-opt them in the Neddy structure, but has so far not succeeded in convincing them. The French system appears to be more conflictual, although President Giscard d'Estaing has, since the 1978 elections, made a point of wooing the moderate elements in the French trade-union movement. Only Germany, of the countries here surveyed, has succeeded in obtaining union consent to the implications of restructuring the industry of the European Community.

Policies under the Iron Lady

The change of government in Britain in 1979, with the election of the Conservative Party under Margaret Thatcher, the 'Iron Lady' as the Soviet press has dubbed her, necessarily implied a change in industrial policy: indeed, one could say that it was one of the dominant themes of the election. A return to 'market realities' was offered as an alternative to continuous subsidisation of bankrupt firms at taxpayers' expense; viable portions of the NEB's portfolio would be sold to the public; government would trim expenditure, reduce public sector borrowing and stop 'crowding out' private borrowers. In short, the British voting public elected a team of people who stated their confidence in the market as an allocator of resources and who promised to reverse the policies of a whole series of previous governments, including past Conservative ones.

Has the promised revolution taken place?

It is difficult to judge so soon (nine months) after the event. The ship of state, like a giant tanker, will continue on its previous course for some time before it begins to show signs of a change of direction. In the United Kingdom one can point to many situations which are a simple projection of the past and which show as yet no sign of radical change: British Leyland asked for, and obtained, more cash; the public sector borrowing requirement did not diminish; the British Steel Corporation continued to make losses and offered no prospects of breaking even by mid-1980; regional aids were cut by a third, but by no means scrapped; Section 8 of the 1972 Industry Act (giving government the power to rescue individual firms anywhere in the country) remained on the statute books, although it was announced that aids would 'be more selectively assessed'[46]; the NEB, butt of many pre-election speeches, continued to exist, albeit with a re-defined role; plans to sell the marketable parts of the state's assets stopped short of disposing of those of the really profitable British National Oil Corporation, although part of the state's shareholding in British Petroleum was sold – more to raise cash than for reasons of economic doctrine.

On the other hand, two really impressive breaks with the past have been made: namely, the abolition of exchange control on 23 October 1979; and the concurrent dismantlement of the Price Commission and with it, the whole philosophy of wage and price control. Both acts of policy bear witness to the Thatcher Goverment's faith in the market process, while the examples of continuity of policy cited above are evidence of the pragmatism with which it presumably intends to bridge – with the help of time – the gap between theory and practice.

Others before the present government, however, have been caught in the trap of side-stepping awkward issues in the name of 'overriding political considerations' and it is legitimate to ask oneself both how much change one can reasonably expect from the Thatcher Government and how far it will in practice dare to go (the two not necessarily being the same).

Before judging how well the Thatcher Government's industrial policy compares with its philosophy, it is important to distinguish between important and secondary issues. The Government would pass the test if it accomplished three tasks:

   (a) if it allowed private firms to collapse if and when bankrupt, and allowed firms to restructure and rationalise if and when necessary;

   (b) if it insisted on nationalised industries turning in, if not a profit, at least no loss; and

   (c) if it decided not to accommodate, with inflation, wage increases in excess of productivity.

Other fascinating but secondary issues, which do not constitute a true test of the Government's will to alter industrial policies fundamentally include:

the role of the NEB in supplementing private venture capital;
marginal changes in the size of the state sector in industry;

the extent of regional aid; and the ending of the state monopoly in telecommunications.

Even if the government only succeeded in accomplishing the first two tasks, and failed to control inflation, this would still be an adequate (although not resounding) practical achievement. Anything less than this, however, would constitute a compromise with reality such that the effective difference between past and present policies would be imperceptible.

The true direction of the Thatcher Government's industrial policy will become apparent all too soon, because its cost in terms of extra unemployment will be considerable, if it remains true to its pre-election promises. Some 52 000 redundancies are forecast for British Steel alone[47] while private failures can be expected to mount as recession in the United States, uncertainty in the world oil market and political instability all take their toll.

It will prove extremely difficult to restore the British Steel Corporation and British Leyland to a break-even position, if only because the Thatcher Government's Olympian policy of non-involvement in the day-to-day running of these two firms is not credible. Everybody knows that the state is not only their owner, but has very deep and well-lined pockets. Trade unions in particular are, not unnaturally, convinced that they can establish direct access to these limitless public funds by simply shaking the tree hard enough. Until these assets are disposed of to private interests or otherwise dismantled, the crippling strike weapon will be brandished and used to extract wages in excess of productivity, thus making it impossible to reach the ever-receding break-even target. There is probably no realistic alternative to de-nationalisation in the long run, although reporting directly to Parliament might conceivably provide the necessary counter-weight.

As for private firms, it may be significant that one could read in the back pages of the *Financial Times*, early in 1980, that 'a further 250 Dunlop jobs are now in jeopardy on Merseyside *following the failure of company talks with the government over grant aid for relocation*'.[48] If this means that Sir Keith Joseph, as Secretary of State for Industry, is prepared to allow industrial restructuring to proceed in spite of considerable loss of jobs in a highly sensitive area, then one can start to talk about a break with the past. The test, however, will come when the process of restructuring accelerates and the rate of unemployment increases still further and provokes still greater unrest. It will then take much courage not to interfere. In these circumstances, the Secretary of State for industry might do worse than consider the policy outlined earlier in Chapter 2: to reform the 1965 Redundancy Payments Act to allow for more generous state funding of severance pay (at present limited to a maximum of £3300) in order to defuse political pressures, without reversing the process of structural adaptation.

Italy: State Capitalism

Italy is an example of industrial policy gone wrong. What is significant, and disturbing, is that in many respects her industrial policy structures are not very different from those of France or Britain.

There are the famous Italian holding companies, the sprawling Istituto Reconstructione Industriale (IRI), the troubled Ente Nationale Idrocarburi (ENI) and other public groups, employing a staggering 30 per cent of the industrial labour force (compared with 10 per cent for France, 15 per cent for Germany and 12 to 14 per cent for Britain[49]). In this respect Italy is unique. But it must be recalled that Italy was catapulted into the modern age by IRI. The logic behind 'state capitalism' was to use a group like IRI as a driving force for the industrialisation of the country.[50] Other countries started after World War II with a damaged but pre-existent private industrial base. Italy started from scratch. State capitalism, however, has proved subject to diminishing returns and, in recent years, extremely vulnerable to political – and other – pressures. Romano Prodi, of the Centro di Economia e Politica Industriale at the University of Bologna, puts it this way:

> The execution of the Italian Government's policy of intervening to support firms in crisis has been almost exclusively in the hands of Italy's public enterprises. In the 1950s these rescue operations were a source of opposition and controversy in the private sector. In the early 1960s such practices came to be tolerated as a part of the legitimate strategy of large industrial groups. By the end of the 1960s and in the beginning of the 1970s they were widely regarded as the only means of avoiding a chain of bankruptcies.[51]

In other words, Italy has travelled down the road which the United Kingdom has only just embarked upon, of co-opting the private sector into supporting state intervention as a matter of course.

As in France, Italy's main banks are nationalised, which means there is no market or parliamentary control over the allocation of a large part of the national savings. Parliament, moreover, prefers to vote large sums to cover the deficits of the state sector, rather than to oblige it to restructure. As long as the inefficiencies of the public sector were minimal, and in great part due to its socially and politically motivated attempts to bring the industrial revolution to the Mezzogiorno, this policy did not endanger the economy of the entire country. Since the oil crisis precipitated in 1973 and the recession, however, Italy's state-owned companies have registered large and growing debts. IRI alone made a loss of $1000 million in 1977 and of $1300 million in 1978, more than half of which was due to steel operations and the Alfa Sud motor car plant. Its accumulated debts amounted to a staggering $21 000 million at the end of 1978.[52] ENI, the state hydrocarbons holding company, also made losses, although not on the same scale as IRI ($420 million in 1978), while Montedison, a 'privately' owned chemical giant with an important state shareholding, halved its $630 million loss in 1977 to just $320 million in 1978, bringing its accumulated losses to some $2200 million. These firms have proved unable to restructure Italy's industry, partly, it must be noted in their defence, because the whole question has become hopelessly politicised. Thus IRI's restructuring plans start from the premise that its 520 000 workforce must be maintained at existing levels. The result is a particularly rapid inflationary spiral as the government automatically extends credit lines to loss-making firms.

In the meantime, the private sector has fared no better and, instead of letting firms go bankrupt, the state sector simply expands by taking them over. A classical example of this was the absorption of Motta and Alemagna by IRI in 1974. These two famous sweet, cake and ice cream firms, financially weakened by a stagnant market and incessant price wars, were saved from collapse by IRI, which decided to merge them into a colossal state-owned food processing conglomerate, Unidal. The merger was one in name only: the trade unions refused to permit Unidal to shut down plants made redundant by the merger, with the result that in its first fifteen months' operation the new firm made a loss of $110 million.[53] In August 1977, having exhausted the patience of its bankers, it turned to its principal shareholder, IRI, for help. At an extraordinary shareholders meeting in September 1977 the liquidation of Unidal was seriously discussed, whereupon the trade unions started a nation-wide dispute. Finally, in the course of 1978, agreement was reached to transfer the viable parts of Unidal to a new firm (SIDALM, Societa Industria Alimentari, Milan) and to reabsorb the 1400 redundant workers into other parts of the IRI empire.[54]

There are, indeed, signs that even IRI cannot continue to take the underwriting of its debts by the state for granted. Early in 1977, its metal manufacturing group, Egam, went bankrupt. Instead of simply allowing the losses to mount, IRI re-organised the group, sold off various bits to private sector buyers, like Fiat, and retained a much slimmed-down operation.[55]

Another attempt at industrial surgery, this time less successful, took place in the summer and autumn of 1977. Societa Generale Immobiliare (SGI), the country's largest private building contractor, had been ruined by the usual combination of unlucky speculation in real estate and a slump in demand for its services. Michele Sindona left Milan for New York under a cloud and his empire was up for sale – if a buyer could be found. SGI's total debts outstanding to banks alone amounted to $580 million (over twice the value of its assets, valued at $200 million) and it was feared that its collapse would have severe repercussions throughout the economy. The Prime Minister, then Julio Andreotti, intervened directly, but even IRI refused to take on this very large and very lame duck. An Italo-American consortium coordinated by John Connally, the former Secretary of the Treasury of the United States, was created. The take-over agreement included the sale by IRI of one of its few profitable firms, Condotte d'Acqua, also in the civil engineering sector. This was an unprecedented step: IRI, instead of automatically absorbing SGI was instead prepared to sacrifice to private interests its own profitable firm. In the event, the agreement, finalised in September 1977, was blocked by the Italian trade unions and opposed by the powerful Communist Party. After months of agonising indecision, a consortium of 39 banks, led by the state-owned Banco di Roma, was formed to take-over the ailing giant.[56] The 'system' had won once again!

A similar, but even larger crisis started to develop in mid-1978 in the chemical industry. The SIR chemicals group (Societa Italiana

Resine), with a majority of its shares in private hands, announced the progressive closure of some of its plants in Sardinia. The Rome Correspondent of the *Financial Times* reported that 'the political consequences of mass lay-offs has forced the Government to intervene and to ask the banks, at least in the short-term, to extend new credits to the chemical groups . . . '.[57] In August 1978, faced with the imminent collapse of SIR, the Government rushed through a bill to stave off bankruptcies. The new law applies to firms with accumulated debts of 50 000 million lira ($45 million) and unable to meet current commitments. According to the new law, in the first instance, a consortium of creditors is to be formed to take over the ailing firm and produce a restructuring plan. If the creditors are unwilling to undertake this thankless task, the Government will appoint a commissioner for it. Only if the latter can produce no viable programme will the company be wound up. The law has since been applied to SIR. Its creditors (mainly banks) finally formed a consortium and produced a restructuring plan calling for 1 000 000 million lira ($1200 million) of government (public) funds. The Italian Senate approved this rescue package as a matter of course in November 1979[58] (by instructive contrast to the uproar caused at exactly the same time, over a comparable sum, by Chrysler's request in the United States for a $1500 million loan from the Administration).

Smaller private companies can, when in trouble, turn to Gestioni Epartci Pazioni Industriali (GEPI), a state-financed source of emergency aid for failing firms. GEPI has so far rescued some 140 of them and asked for $2400 million over 1979–81 to keep them alive.[59]

Italy is living off her capital and her leaders, on both sides of industry, are well aware of it. Even Luciano Lama, the leader of Italy's largest, Communist-dominated trade union, the Conferazione Generale Italiano Lavoratori, has admitted that Italian workers will have to make 'substantial sacrifices' in order to 'stimulate investment in industry'.[60] But the rank and file refuses to follow and the consequences show up in Table 3.1.

The crisis in Italy's political system has spilled over with disastrous effect, into the economic sphere. It is perhaps significant that Italy does not seem to have a Neddy along British lines, or a 'concerted action' process along German lines; that is, she does not have a place where both sides of industry can meet under the chairmanship of the government to try to find mutually acceptable solutions to what are

Table 3.1
A Striking Loss (work days lost in labour conflicts per 1000 workers)

	Average 1976/77	Trend 1977/78
Italy	1 880	→
Ireland	970	↑
United Kingdom	700	↑
France[a]	350	↗
Belgium	325	→
Denmark[b]	300	↓
Germany	35	↑
Netherlands	5	→

Source: *Vision*, Paris, February 1978, p. 25., with modification of 1977/78 trend to include the first six months of 1978.

[a] Excluding 'general' strikes
[b] Industry only.

undoubtedly very ticklish political problems. Such a tripartite structure cannot in fact be transposed to Italy because the state (the government) is, itself, the single largest employer of the industrial workforce. As such it enters inevitably into employer – employee conflicts while at the same time seeking re-election. This convergence of economic and political functions in the Italian state will have fairly predictable negative consequences for Italian democracy in the longer run and for the Italian economy immediately.

Italy is a good example of the economic and political dynamics of state capitalism and the systematic rejection of the market as an allocator of the nation's resources. Once the role of the state in the economy becomes too large, the slightest economic decision, dictated by the most obvious common sense, becomes hopelessly politicised. The ensuing breakdown of the economy then constitutes an obvious danger to political liberties in its own right. The 'intelligent radical' tends to minimise this threat: the all-wise government will know when to stop and state intervention will never be pushed to its logical extreme. Italy, however, is not far from it and there is nothing in the dynamics of industrial policy, apart from frequently feeble parliamentary control and hortative European Community guidelines, to stop the process from snowballing.

The Netherlands: Third World Considerations

The Netherlands has the type of industrial policy which combines government support for industry – under certain conditions – with a positive attitude to international trade and structural change.

State enterprises are relatively unimportant: in employment terms, they account for a mere 3.6 per cent of the working population, or 10 per cent of the industrial work force. The Netherlands, in fact, is a concrete example of the northern European model of socialism at work, namely to let private industry produce the wealth and to let the state redistribute that wealth. Nationalisation of private assets for reasons of political doctrine is unknown and very rare for reasons of economic necessity. But the temptation to take a hand in the geographic allocation of resources and in the restructuring process has proved irresistible, and the Netherlands has a very comprehensive and well-endowed industrial policy. Because of its free trade tradition, it provides one of the very rare instances in Western Europe of a conscious attempt to formulate a positive industrial policy. It epitomises the 'intelligent radical's' approach to state intervention.

Dutch industrial policy has two long-term objectives: to improve the distribution of industrial activity throughout the country, on the one hand, and to re-structure Dutch industry, on the other. For the purpose of the first objective, the Netherlands is divided into three zones: the Randstad (the provinces of Zuid-Holland, Noord-Holland and the area around Utrecht); the extreme north and extreme south; and the remainder. There are positive disincentives to investment in the Randstad, which take the form of a tax on new investment; investments in the least developed outlying areas are encouraged by a system of special regional subsidies of up to 31 per cent; and investments in the remaining intermediate area are promoted by means of various premia, which can be cumulative, and which are given according to various criteria. In addition to a basic investment premium, extra points can be earned if the investment is directed to certain 'growth towns', is non-polluting, improves the 'quality of life' or is involved in the production of goods which do not compete with developing countries.

This last point shows that the Dutch government is attempting to accommodate developing-country trade in a positive manner. It may prove difficult in practice to distinguish between developing-country-type goods and developed-country products in the future, but the aim is laudable and corresponds to the image the Netherlands has as the champion of developing-country interests in the European Community and as a traditionally open economy.

The new Dutch industrial policy also serves short-term emergency purposes. There is a system of aid to individual companies in short-term difficulties which can obtain loans from the state (at commercial rates of interest, but in amounts exceeding what banks would be prepared to lend) to ease a cash-flow crisis. This system is designed to prevent bankruptcies from occurring among normally healthy firms and thereby to save both firms and jobs from needless destruction. The objective is again admirable, but it may prove difficult in practice to distinguish between structual and cyclical difficulties. The trouble with the systematic prevention of bankruptcies in times of cyclical downturn is that the economy may end up with a series of lame ducks which will offer fewer new jobs when the economy picks up again.

The restructuring of Dutch industry is helped by a public body Nederlandse Herstructureringsmaatschappij (NEHEM), which provides investment aid to sectors with long-term problems. It only provides such aid if a detailed restructuring plan has been drawn up and agreed to by the firm and, presumably, the workforce. Where redundancies are inevitable, the Government attempts to channel new private investment in their direction and, if this is not forthcoming, will step up government expenditure on infrastructure projects. The purpose of this type of aid is to make the industry competitive rather than merely to keep it alive. It has been applied already to the shipbuilding, foundry and textile industries.

Part of the success in restructuring Dutch industry no doubt stems from the generous social insurance benefits upon which redundant workers can fall back if they wish. In addition, little stigma attaches to those who voluntarily withdraw from the active labour force and live on the dole.

The money for these expensive aid schemes – amounting to some 5000 million guilders a year (excluding personal income transfers) – comes, of course, from natural gas. Britain and Norway take note! Indeed, if Dutch industrial policy were to stop there it would be an outstanding example of what the 'intelligent radical's' policies (lubricated with sufficient funds) can do to help the restructuring process. It is, however, accompanied by a deep-rooted hostility to big business, doubtless springing from the overwhelming presence of a huge multinational – Philips – in a very small economy. Profits are considered to be a scandal rather than the normal reward to the efficient and imaginative firm. A scheme for taxing so-called 'excess' profits has therefore been under discussion for some years in the Netherlands and has been presented to Parliament not, it should be noted, by a socialist, but by a centre-right government. The purpose is to encourage small business at the expense of large. But there is a danger that the progressive taxation of firms will diminish the market incentive to achieve maximum efficiency. In the longer term, it will reduce the propensity to invest in the country, will encourage capital exports and will discourage capital imports. Finally, taxing away 'excess' profits blunts the market signal to invest more in the industry where they occur, causing bottlenecks and, in an open economy such as the Netherlands, imports will make up for lost production. This scheme will thus place an extra burden on the restructuring process of Dutch industry which otherwise would have had a better chance of success.

European Community: Small and Growing Role

Nine-tenths of all industrial policy in the European Community takes place at the national level, but a small and growing role is now reserved to the Community authorities.

Under Article 92 of the Treaty of Rome, state aids which distort competition 'by favouring certain enterprises or certain productions' are outlawed. Regional aids and aids to promote 'important projects of common European interest or to remedy a serious disturbance', however, are permitted under certain conditions.

The Commission of the European Community supervises all members' aid systems to ensure that they fall within the permitted limits. It has three objectives:

    (a) to make sure that aids do not distort competition within the Community;

    (b) to encourage a better distribution of industrial activity within the Common Market; and

    (c) to promote the rationalisation of production in declining sectors or sectors subject to intense competition.

The Commission has been fighting a long-standing battle for 'transparency' of aid systems, for it is not enough for member states to notify the Commission of their various schemes: in order to estimate their impact, one has to know how much they amount to in quantitative terms. The Commission therefore limits the right of members to offer 'opaque' aids, such as subsidised electricity or freight rates, certain aids linked to employment rather than invest- ment or exemptions from property taxes. It far prefers aids expressed as a certain percentage of the value of an investment or (since 1979) in currency units per job. Furthermore the Commission sets limits to the amount of 'transparent' aids members may give to industry.

Regional Policy

The Commission's regional policy developed in three stages during the 1970s.

1. In 1971 it issued guidelines warning member states that aids in excess of 20 per cent in 'central' regions would be considered as distorting competition within the Common Market and that aids in excess of 20 per cent in 'peripheral' regions would be scrutinised for their job-displacement effects.[61]

2. In 1975, the Commission's regional policy became clearer – and more accommodating – in that the 20 per cent ceiling was raised for all but the most prosperous regions. The European Community was divided into four zones, ranging from the highly assisted to 'general' zones. Only in the highly assisted zones (Berlin, the Mezzogiorno and Northern Ireland) was the ceiling of aid-intensity left open to *ad hoc* negotiation: in other zones, ceilings ranged from 30, 25 and 20 per cent respectively. The Commission emphasised that these ceilings represented maxima, which it hoped would not be necessary to use, and that the longer-term aim was to reduce the level of aids as much as possible.[62] Needless to say, the Commission's policy was only adopted after months of high-level consultation with member states; it may be safely assumed that the end result corresponded roughly to the situation as it stood in 1975.

3. In 1979 new guidelines were introduced.[63] For the first time a 75 per cent ceiling was agreed upon for the highly assisted areas and ceilings were raised for other areas (see summary in Table 3.2).

The Commission re-emphasised that the new ceilings constituted an 'absolute maximum'; and as far as aids in the general zone were concerned, the Commission added hopefully that 'for this cate- gory the trend must be towards a reduction on the level of aids as

Table 3.2

Stages in the Development of the European Community's Regional Policy

	European Community's regional aid grid		Permitted subsidy as % of investment	
	Highly assisted areas	Assisted areas	Intermediate areas	General (other) areas
1971 Guidelines			20%	20%
	(no clear ceiling outside 'central' areas)			
1975 Guidelines		30%	25%	20%
1979 Guidelines	75%	40%	30%	25%

Source: *Report on Competition Policy*, Commission of the European Community, Brussels, various issues.

far as possible'.[64] Greenland and Ireland continued to be treated as 'special cases', and Italy continued to introduce stop-gap and operational aid schemes in favour of the south to which the Commission continued to object.

One has the definite impression that in the European Community the Commission, far from setting limits on member states' actions, has some difficulty in keeping pace with them. One awaits the next regional aid revision (in 1982) with interest.

Sectoral Policy

Besides attempting to coordinate regional policy in the European Community, the Commission also supervises sectoral policies in shipbuilding, steel, textiles and footwear. In May 1978, it published a policy document, where it laid down the guiding principles for examining sectoral aids, of which the most important were clearly (i) that 'industrial problems and unemployment should not be transferred from one Member State to another' and (ii) that aids should *resolve* problems rather than preserve the *status quo*.[65]

It is difficult to judge whether these criteria impose effective limits on the nature of selective state aids in member states or whether they are merely exhortative. The successive directives for shipbuilding (see below) show an even greater escalation in permitted aid-intensity than occurred even with regional policy. Furthermore, the overall level of aid to sectors in difficulty is distorted in the case of steel and textiles because the Commission itself has introduced indirect (and highly opaque) measures of support, such as non-tariff protection and internal 'orderly marketing' arrangements.

Other Aid Schemes

Besides regional and sectoral aid programmes, member countries of the European Community operate a number of widely divergent aid schemes, ranging from the most general (such as across-the-board export credit subsidisation) to the most specific (such as discretionary grants to save failing firms). These 'general' aid schemes have so far defeated the Commission's attempts to devise a coherent Community policy with regard to them.

Instead, the Commission requires the notification of all cases (and keeps an eye on the official gazettes of member countries to make sure that no aids pass unnoticed) and examines them on their individual merits, in the light of the general principles already outlined. In 1977 the Commission for the first time published information on the number of cases thus examined and gave a country and sector breakdown, continuing the practice in 1978 (see Table 3.3 below).

Table 3.3

Number of Non-regional and Non-sectoral Aids to Industry in the European Community Examined by the Commission in 1978 (1977).

Sector	Member state					Total	
	Belgium	Germany (FR)	France	Nether-lands	United King-dom	1978	(1977)
Chemicals	1			1	8	10	(8)
Engineering and metals	2			1	2	5	(8)
Vehicles	1			1	2	4	
Textiles and clothing	1			2		3	(3)
Other	2	2	1	2	1	8	(20)
Total 1978	7	2	1	7	13	30	
(Total 1977)	(10)	(0)	(2)	(0)	(12)		(39)

Source: *Report on Competition Policy*, 7th and 8th reports, Commission of the European Community, Brussels, paragraphs 223 and 219 respectively.

From this it was learnt that 39 significant cases were notified in 1977 of which 4 were considered to be incompatible with Common Market obligations. One of these concerned the British Export Credits Guarantee Department (ECGD) which offered subsidised loans for British exports to the rest of the European Community. Protracted negotiations ensued, in which the Commission rejected at least one British modification as still being 'tantamount to state aid'.[66] The British Government finally discontinued its export credit subsidies on exports to the Community on 1 April 1978. A comparable scheme operated by the French Government to stimulate investment in the export sector was objected to and discontinued in November 1978.

Another notable victory for the Commission was the reduction and containment of the British temporary employment subsidy (TES). The TES was introduced in 1975 and was paid to employers who kept on workers who would otherwise have lost their jobs. It could be paid for three months and extended a further three months if necessary. The recipients had to be sound firms which were in a position to offer good prospects of permanent non-subsidised jobs. In that form it was approved by the Commission of the European Community.[67]

By 1977 the scheme had been extended several times. Its initial budget of £6 million had been raised to £431 million and the length of time that the subsidy could be paid extended to eighteen months.[68] What bothered the Commission, however, and gave rise to complaints on the part of other member countries of the European Community was the fact that over half that aid was going to support employment in the textile industry – which was equally hard hit in other member states – and it was not linked to any plan for restructuring the recipient firms. As the Commission remarked, the TES 'enables certain industries with excess capacity to carry on with uncompetitive production'.[69] This, it was judged, had two undesirable consequences:

(a) it did not solve the problems of the recipient firms and
(b) it exerted a depressive influence on competing firms not receiving such subsidies (the so-called 'displacement effect').

As a result of pressure within the European Community, the British Government introduced 'sector limits' (in order to stop TES-related aid from building up in the textile industry) and reduced the volume of aid quite substantially (total committed expenditure up to the end of 1978 amounting to only £54 million).[70] Furthermore, the

Commission's monitoring system forced the British Government to withdraw six cases which the Commission deemed 'unacceptable'.

In short, the Commission of the European Community appears to be stricter with 'general' aids than with those which fall clearly into one or other of the 'official' categories of regional or sectoral support systems. It has several notable victories to its credit and its efforts to enforce some discipline on wayward member countries cannot be totally discounted.

What can be criticised, however, is the Commission's basically extremely conciliatory and accommodating attitude to state aids to industry generally. It does not question the basic premise that state aids to industry can help the restructuring process without introducing serious inefficiencies and distortions in allocation. As a result, it is able to accept all but the most blatant forms of stop-gap assistance as being of some use – somehow.

It is for instance to be deplored that in December 1979 the Commission departed from its former rule of using only fixed investments as the criterion for judging the compatibility of aid systems with Common Market obligations and introduced numbers of jobs as an alternative denominator (albeit within an absolute limit expressed as a percentage of investment in more prosperous regions). This softening of the guidelines meant that member countries became free to stimulate labour-intensive industries in highly-assisted areas and to stimulate labour-intensive service activities anywhere.[71]

The Commission of the European Community is certainly in a position to make life difficult for governments in the matter of state aids. It is a pity that it has, on the whole, been rather accommodating.

Two further aspects of industrial policy have a European Community-wide dimension, namely trade and competition policy.

Trade Policy

Member countries of the European Community have delegated certain instruments of policy to the Commission in order to create the Common Market. Among the most important, from the point of view of industrial policy, is trade policy. The Community is entrusted with negotiating the conditions of entry for imports from all over the world. It handles anti-dumping actions, negotiates self-limitation agreements and negotiates tariff rates with its principal trade partners. To the extent that an industry's troubles can be traced to severe import competition, it is within the power of the Commission, armed with a mandate from the Council of Ministers, to negotiate some form of protection for Community firms. It has already done so for steel, ballbearings and textiles and may also do so for other troubled sectors, such as fibres or plastics. But this policy has its problems.

By altering the conditions upon which imports enter the European Community it runs the risk of retaliation. In order to minimise this risk, the new level of protection has to be negotiated with its trading partners. The latter are only too conscious of the fact that the Community usually represents their largest market, while they represent a negligible fraction of the Community's total exports. They can, therefore, be expected to 'understand' the Community's need for extra protection – but will usually insist that it should be strictly temporary. Whether or not it actually turns out to be temporary is another matter and depends on the circumstances in each case. As will be discussed in the following chapter, the Community's retreat from liberal trade policies in selected sectors shows all the symptoms of a negative industrial policy.

Competition Policy

The Directorate-General for Industrial Affairs in the Commission of the European Community, under the leadership of Viscount Etienne Davignon, as the Commissioner, has been in the limelight because of the Community's well-publicised 'crisis cartel' for steel (see below). The question immediately arose as to whether other sectors plagued by over-capacity and with suitably oligopolistic structures could not also avoid some of the consequences of the recession by making reciprocal and mutually beneficial agreements to cut down on capacity and limit production.

The lawyers in the Directorate-General for Competition Policy were duly consulted. The steel cartel was governed by the Treaty of Paris, which provided for such emergency measures in cases of 'manifest crisis', but cartels in other industries would fall under the Treaty of Rome. Careful examination of Article 85 by the Competition Directorate-General, however, failed to reveal an escape clause which would permit the formation of a crisis cartel. This was particularly irritating for the Directorate-General for Industrial Affairs which had invested a considerable amount of time and effort in persuading the nine principal European synthetic fibre producers to enter into an agreement for the 'orderly reduction of capacity' and for the introduction of a production and sales quota system. The agreement was notified in July 1978.[72] The Commission's Competition Directorate-General objected especially to the production and sales quotas and the parties were asked to submit a modified text. In January 1980 negotiations were broken off: the Competition Directorate-General still objected to the arrangement and the parties decided to withdraw their application for clearance.

The rigorous attitude of the Competition Directorate with regard to private 'orderly' restructuring arrangements stands by contrast to its more conciliatory attitude to public 'orderly' structural policies. The reason is not difficult to see: on the one hand, it has to bend private firms to its will; on the other, it has to bend to the will of states. The difference in views between the Directorate-General for Industrial Affairs and the Directorate-General for Competition is also intriguing.

Other Instruments of Industrial Policy

Besides the supervision of state aids, trade and competition policy, the European Community has several more instruments of industrial policy at its disposal. The European Social Fund provides help for retraining workers made redundant by the creation of the Common Market, but it has always been kept notoriously short of money and is unable to be of much help. Its statutes were amended in 1972 in order to make it more flexible, in particular by allowing it to respond to requests for retraining aid from the private as well as from the public sector; and by giving it a definite regional bias.

The European Investment Bank provides loans or loan-guarantees to further regional policies, to restructure industry or to promote new activities. It, too, has a strong regional bias and Italy is the principal recipient of such loans.

The European Regional Fund provides outright subsidies to regional projects in member states, but it always does so in conjunction with an equivalent, or larger, national subsidy. The amount of money which the Commission has at its disposal to spend on industrial policy has been estimated to amount to no more than one per cent of what member states spend individually. Since January 1978, the European Community has been given the green light to borrow up to $3000 million on the long-term Euro-currency market which could be used to finance industrial adaptation projects. This scheme has yet to get under way, but when it does it will be the largest of the Community's financial instruments of industrial policy.

The principal virtue of the European Community is to remind member states that they are not islands, sufficient unto themselves. Just as great strides have been made in most countries to improve communications between employers and employees, so it is equally necessary to create similar channels of communication between interdependent states on industrial policy matters.

NOTES

1. Charles-Albert Michalet, 'France', in Vernon (ed.), *Big Business*, op. cit., p. 113.

2. *Ibid.*

3. *Investment, Licensing and Trade Conditions Abroad: France* (New York: Business International, 1978) p. 5.

4. François de Witt, 'La Croix–Rouge des Entreprises', *L'Expansion*, Paris, April 1978, pp. 100–3.

5. *Ibid.*, p. 102. Translation: 'They do not know their unit costs and therefore they crash without even knowing it.'

6. *Ibid.*, p. 102. Translation: 'We provide the "extra something" which makes the mayonnaise take . . .'

7. David Curry, 'A Bracing Freedom for French Industry', *Financial Times*, 19 May 1978, p. 22.

8. *Ibid.*

9. *L'Expansion*, April 1978, p. 20.

10. *Ibid.*

11. Reported by David Curry, *op. cit.*, p. 22.

12. *The Economist*, 3 June 1978, p. 96.

13. *Le Monde*, Paris, 2 June 1978, p. 1.

14. *Financial Times*, 15 March 1979, p. 20.

15. *Quarterly Economic Review, France*, Economist Intelligence Unit, London, no. 1, 1977, p. 9.

16. Adrian Crawley, *The Rise of Western Germany, 1945–72* (London: Collins, 1973) p. 159.

17. Georg H. Küster, 'Germany', in Vernon (ed.), *Big Business, op. cit.*, pp. 64–86 (at p. 65).

18. Andrew Shonfield, *Modern Capitalism* (London: Oxford University Press, 1965) p. 240, quoted in Küster, *op. cit.*

19. Küster, *op. cit.*, p. 80 (figures for 1966).

20. *Ibid.*, pp. 71–72.

21. *Fifth Report on Competition Policy* (Brussels: Commission of the European Community, 1975) p. 70.

22. *Annual Reports on Competition Policy in OECD Member Countries* (Paris: OECD Secretariat, 1977) pp. 40–41.

23. *Quarterly Economic Review, Federal Republic of Germany* Economist Intelligence Unit, London, no. 2, 1975, p. 11.

24. *The Economist*, 13 December 1975, pp. 88–90.

25. *Financial Times*, 13 June 1978, p. 2.

26. *Le Monde*, 27 May 1978, p. 9.

27. *The Economist*, 3 March 1979, p. 67.

28. 'Opinions are Split on the Virtue of German Banking', *Financial Times*, 14 March 1978, p. 13.

29. *Financial Times*, 4 December 1979, p. 21.

30. *Financial Times*, 14 March 1978, p. 13.

31. *L'Expansion*, April 1978, p. 102.

32. This section was drafted before the general election in Britain in May 1979. Rather than revise the section, trying to take into account the policy changes promised by the new Government, it was decided to add some passages at the end of the section on the Thatcher Government's approach to industrial policy.

33. Littlechild, *op. cit.*, p. 68.

34. *Financial Times*, 14 March 1978, p. 7. In journalistic parlance, Whitehall is shorthand for government departments, whereas Millbank (which is a street that is almost, on the other side of Parliament Square, a continuation of Whitehall, which is also a street) is shorthand for the National Economic Development Office where government, management and labour are brought together.

35. *The National Enterprise Board* (London: Department of Industry, 1977) p. 5.

36. *Sixth Report on Competition Policy* (Brussels: Commission of the European Community, 1978) p. 163.

37 Full-page advertisements in the *Financial Times* by the ICFC ('the smaller business's biggest source of long-term money', *Financial Times*, 21 June 1978, p. 21) show that there is no shortage of venture capital. What *is* in short supply is the adventurous entrepreneur.

38. *Financial Times*, 31 May 1978, p. 8.

39. *Annual Report, Industry Act 1972* (London: Department of Industry, 1975).

40. *Ibid.*, p. 9. The sectors are wool textiles, ferrous foundries, machine tools, paper and board, non-ferrous foundries, electronic components, textile machinery, poultry meat, red meat processing and off-shore supplies to the North Sea oil industry.

41. *Ibid.*, Chairman's Report, p. 20.

42. *Financial Times*, 12 May 1978, p. 14.

43. *Financial Times*, 9 May 1978, p. 7.

44. 'Public Sector Enterprise', *The Economist*, 30 December 1978, p. 41.

45. *Financial Times*, 1 January 1978, p. 8.

46. *Financial Times*, 18 July 1979, p. 1.

47. *Financial Times*, 1 December 1979, p. 1.

48. *Financial Times*, 15 January 1980, p. 8 (italics supplied).

49. These figures are to be found in *Vision*, Paris, February 1978, p. 19, with a slight upward correction for Britain to take account of the nationalisation of the shipbuilding industry. Note that public-sector *industrial* employment is being related to total *industrial* employment. This accounts for the high ratios and highlights the Italian position. If one relates public-sector employment to the total working population, the ratios are much lower. Countries' definitions of

Table 3.4

Breakdown of Public Employees in the Working Population of Selected Countries in the European Community

	Public enterprises (generating revenue) %	Civil servants (pure adminis- tration) %	Total % of working population
Belgium	5.2	16.0	21.2
Britain	8.1	21.3	29.4
Denmark	3.4	17.8	21.2
France	7.3	14.6	21.9
Germany (FR)	7.2	14.3	21.5
Holland	3.6	14.3	17.9
Italy	6.6	12.8	19.4

Source: *The Economist*, London, 30 December 1978, p.40, and 22 December 1979, p. 36.

public-sector employment vary and there is surprisingly little comparable information on the subject. Increasing interest in problems of living with a vast and growing state apparatus has, however, prompted further research. A combination of surveys undertaken by *L'Expansion* and *The Economist* provides the breakdown shown in Table 3.4.

50. *Financial Times*, 4 April 1978, p. 20.

51. Romano Prodi, 'Italy', in Vernon (ed.), *Big Business, op. cit.*, p. 49.

52. *Quarterly Economic Review*, Economist Intelligence Unit, London, no. 2, 1979, p. 14.

53. *The Economist*, 8 October 1977, p. 98.

54. IRI Annual Report 1977 (Rome: IRI, 1978) p. 25–26.

55. *Le Figaro*, Paris, 2 October 1977, p. 6.

56. *Financial Times*, 10 March 1978, p. 78.

57. *Financial Times*, 5 June 1978, p. 2.

58. *Financial Times*, 8 November 1979, p. 21.

59. *The Economist*, 8 December 1979.

60. *La Suisse*, Geneva, 26 January 1978.

61. *Premier rapport sur la politique de concurrence* (Brussels: Commission of the European Community, 1972) para. 149.

62. *Fifth Report on Competition Policy, op. cit.*, paras 85–7.

63. *Eighth Report on Competition Policy* (Brussels: Commission of the European Community, 1979) paras 151–56.

64. *Ibid.*, para. 153.

65. *Ibid.*, para. 176.

66. *Ibid.*, para. 222.

67. *Seventh Report on Competition Policy* (Brussels: Commission of the European Community, 1978) paras 237–41.

68. *Ibid.*, para. 237.

69. *Ibid.*, para. 239.

70. *Eighth Report on Competition Policy, op. cit.*, para. 234.

71. *Ibid.*, para. 152.

72. *Ibid.*, para. 42. For a careful legal analysis of the Davignon Plan and the 'synthetic fibres' episode, see René Joliet, 'Competition, Dirigism and Cartelisation in the European Community'. *The World Economy*, January 1981.

CHAPTER FOUR

Sectoral Problems: Steel, Shipbuilding, Chemicals and Textiles

In recent years, since the early 1970s, several industries in Western Europe have experienced poor demand conditions which cannot be entirely attributed to the slowdown in growth in the world economy. They are the victims of structural change, part of the normal process of growth, whereby some sectors expand as others contract. During the 'recession', their problems have grown so much that their very future is in doubt. Public attention is focussed on their plight to such an extent that the counterpart existence of growing industries is ignored or forgotten.

Structural disease takes various forms – mild, chronic, acute, serious – and occasionally it proves to be fatal. Identified viruses include import competition from Japan and advanced developing countries, which can often cause a very serious condition, but which is rarely completely lethal. Victims of serious forms of structural disease frequently take refuge behind this foreign agent, preferring to gloss over shortcomings that are closer to home. They include: (i) over-capacity, or under-employment of resources, due to unfortunate past investment decisions (the troubles of the petro-chemical industry apparently being largely due to this, giving rise to an acute, but strictly temporary form of the disease); (ii) poor management (for which cures are readily available); (iii) rapid technological change which reduces or annihilates demand for a product overnight (the death of the slide rule being a case in point), the condition being usually fatal, wiping out the economic usefulness of capital goods at a blow; (iv) a change in consumer tastes (for instance, the shift in demand in favour of natural and against synthetic fibres, or away from sugar and butter to lean meat and fruit); (v) a change in relative prices of inputs (for instance oil) which can make nonsense of past investment decisions; (vi) a change in prices of substitute products (for instance, cheap air travel is behind the decline and fall of the luxury transatlantic liner) – and so on. The causes of structural change are extremely varied.

Whatever the cause may be, if the case is serious and involves the potential loss of many jobs, the government is under irresistible pressure to keep the patient alive at almost any cost. Yet it is important, even when bowing to strong political winds, to know the root cause of the disease, whether it can be cured or not and, if so, at what price. If a firm's difficulties are due to reversible factors, such as bad luck, faulty management, past mistakes or a change in government policy, it will either cure itself or be taken over and there is no valid case for public support. If the causes of its difficulties are of a non-reversible kind, such as technological change, growth in other countries or relative price changes, then the only viable alternative to death (fast or slow) is *change*. Therefore, industrial policies, if any, should seek to promote, and not to prevent, change.

The sectors discussed below present symptoms of serious long-term structural disease due mainly to factors of a non-reversible nature: increased import competition, sluggish domestic demand, technological change and relative price changes, to name only a few. The policies adopted by various governments will be discussed in the light of whether or not they help or hinder the process of change.

Steel: Import Restrictions and Export Subsidies

Steel is such a basic industrial input that it cannot help being affected by general business conditions. From 1973–79 there was virtually no growth in industrial production in Western Europe. Government spending on infrastructure projects (large consumers of steel) was cut back which meant that steel mills could not look to home markets to absorb the extra production which was just coming on stream as a result of investment decisions taken before 1973. The European Community, however, is a traditional exporter of steel (for every dollar's worth of imported steel, the Community exported $2.42 in 1972 and $2.90 in 1978) so Community producers could hope to find the markets they needed abroad, especially in OPEC and developing countries, which throughout this period enjoyed an average growth of 6 per cent per annum. Exports of steel from the Community (excluding intra-area trade) in fact rose from $4690 million in 1972, to \$14310 million in 1978 while EFTA steel exports rose from \$1140 million to \$3560 million over the same period of time. Principal third-country export markets in 1978, in order of importance, were the Eastern bloc countries, North America, the OPEC countries and oil-importing developing countries.

Despite this impressive export performance (partly, it must be admitted, helped by subsidies) producers in the European Community have not maintained their market shares abroad. Their share of imports by the United States, for instance, declined from 38 to 31 per cent and in OPEC imports from 38 to 33 per cent (see Table 4.1).

Table 4.1

Share of the European Community in Iron and Steel of its Principal Export Markets, 1973–78. (percentage)

	United States	EFTA	Eastern Europe	Oil-importing LDCs	Oil-exporting LDCs
1973	38	65	34	24	38
1978	31	66	30[a]	22[a]	33

Source: *International Trade 1978–79* (Geneva: GATT Secretariat, 1979) appendices.
[a] 1977.

On a global scale, the European Community's share in world steel trade taken as a whole (but excluding intra-community trade) fell from 31 per cent in 1972 to 27 per cent in 1976.[1] Japan's share of world steel exports increased from 24 per cent to 30 per cent over the same period, while the combined share of Australia, South Africa, India, South Korea and Brazil rose from 2 to 5 per cent. The increased shares of Japan and these five countries more than account for the fall in the Community's share of world steel trade. In spite of this unfavourable global trend, the Community remains a strong net exporter of steel, a paradox which can only be explained by the presence of import restrictions, on the one hand, and (indirect) export subsidies, on the other. In fact, imports still stand at less than half the value of exports, and the Community's balance of trade in steel actually improved from 1972 to 1976 (see Table 4.2).

The extent of direct and indirect subsidies can be inferred from the fact that all steel producers of any size in the European Community have been losing money. They lost nearly \$3000 million

Table 4.2
European Community's Balance of Trade in Iron and Steel ($'000 million)

Bilateral balances with	1972	1976	1978
North America	+1.06	+0.85	+2.17
Other West European Countries	+1.48	+2.53	+0.19
Japan	−0.31	−0.59	−0.36
Australia, New Zealand and South Africa	−0.01	−2.10	−0.8
Eastern trading area	+0.48	+2.37	+3.03
Oil-exporting LDCs	+0.37	+1.41	+2.35
Oil-importing LDCs	+0.63	+0.96	+2.02
Other countries	−0.95	−0.15	−0.2
	+2.75	+5.28	+9.30

Source: *International Trade 1978–79* (Geneva: GATT Secretariat, 1979).

in 1977[2] and fared no better in 1978. The French firms Sacilor and Usinor lost most per tonne of steel produced, followed by Britain's BSC, Italy's Italsider and Belgium's Cockerill. West German firms did somewhat better, but even they made losses of $20 per tonne of steel produced (see Table 4.3). Such losses cannot be sustained for any length of time even by state-owned steel companies and even less by privately-owned ones. For this reason governments and steel producers have given their reluctant support to the Davignon Plan.

Table 4.3
Performance of the European Community's Big Steel Producers, 1977

Firm	Country	Losses per tonne
Salzgitter	West Germany	−$20
Arbed	Luxemburg	−$20
Estel	West Germany and Netherlands	−$24
Klockner	West Germany	−$39
Cockerill	Belgium	−$44
BSC	United Kingdom	−$46
Italsider	Italy	−$46
Usinor	France	−$54
Sacilor	France	−$78

Source: *Financial Times*, London, 5 July 1978, p. 16.

The Davignon Plan is named after the European Community's Commissioner for Industrial Affairs who introduced it, namely Viscount Etienne Davignon, and was initially composed of three basic elements: (i) voluntary production quotas, (ii) compulsory minimum prices and (iii) import restrictions. Together, these three measures were designed to bring supply and demand for steel into equilibrium at a price which would cover the cost of production at the Community's more efficient plants. Each element of the plan as it now stands, at the time of writing, was introduced separately, the most recent addition being compulsory production quotas, introduced in October 1980. The Commission is discovering at first hand the joys of trying to run a cartel in a declining market.[3]

The Commission of the European Community started early in 1977 with 'voluntary' quotas on production for major Community steel producers in order to harden depressed steel prices. By May 1977 the Commission felt that the market was ready for the introduction of voluntary 'guideline' prices for certain steel products, such as sheet and coil, and compulsory minimum prices for steel reinforcing bars used in construction. (This distinction was presumably made so as not to penalise unduly the steel-using traded-goods sector, and to make the non-traded goods sector (that is, the construction industry) bear the brunt of the higher prices).

This first attempt at running the European Community's steel-market did not prove successful. Foreign producers continued to supply the Community at prices below the guidelines, which forced steel producers to break the guidelines themselves. Many of them exceeded their production quotas and some of them sold below agreed prices (Usinor, for instance, was fined in July 1978 for having done so), not to speak of the now famous Bresciani, who are not members of Eurofer (the big steel producers' club, set up under the wing of the Commission of the Community) and who ignored the Community's 'voluntary' production and price guidelines, as well as the compulsory prices for construction steel.

In January 1978 the Commission of the European Community therefore reinforced its measures. It introduced a minimum-price system for steel imports, partly to forestall the diversion to the Community of steel intended for the United States, following the introduction there of the 'trigger-price mechanism' in November 1977.[4] The Community's minimum-price system effectively obliged steel importers to respect its floor prices or pay a duty which would force them up to that level. It implied, in effect, a variable levy on steel imports and as such required the renegotiation of trade agreements with the Community's principal steel suppliers. The first half of 1978 saw voluntary restraint and minimum-price agreements negotiated with EFTA, the Comecon countries, Spain, Japan, Brazil, South Africa, South Korea and, after a great deal of arm-twisting, Australia. These agreements were originally concluded only up to the end of 1978, but they have since been extended.

At the same time as the Commission of the European Community introduced its trigger-price mechanism, it raised its guideline prices by 5 per cent. As a result, steel prices improved slightly in the first months of the year – but the Bresciani still had to be brought to heel. They had taken advantage of the price and quantity restraints agreed to by their larger brethren by expanding production and lowering prices. Being small, privately owned and profitable, they were beholden to no one and proved largely immune to government and Community pressure. They were also very numerous – 81 in all – and the first rule of successful cartel-building is to avoid fragmented industries. They were finally brought to book for having ignored the *compulsory* prices for construction steels. Four of them were fined and two weeks later they agreed to channel their exports through a single sales agency which would be run with the help of Community staff.[5] They also agreed to cut back their steel exports to other Community countries by half to their former levels.

Having brought the Bresciani under control, the Commission of the European Community announced another 'voluntary' reduction in production for the third quarter of 1978[6] and strengthened its import controls by announcing that steel cargoes which did not respect Community prices would be fined up to 25 per cent of their value. As a result of this complex of measures, steel prices rose between 20–25 per cent in 1978.[7]

'Discipline', however, proved increasingly difficult to maintain in a recession-bound market.[8] By mid-1980, steel prices had fallen by 13 per cent and output had dropped catastrophically in Britain (down 56 per cent), Denmark (35 per cent) and Belgium (30 per cent). Conditions were described as 'chaotic' as steel firms 'resorted to frantic price-cutting to grab a share of the shrinking market': losses amounted to $20 million a day.[9] But help was at hand, in the shape of a greatly reinforced Davignon Plan (Mark II), which introduced compulsory production quotas under the emergency provisions of Article 58 of the Treaty of Paris, as from October 1980.

The compulsory quota system covered 80 per cent of all steel production and more than 300 firms, all of which were required to send in a *daily* production report by telex to the European Community's central computer. Unused quotas could be sold among firms and the arrangement was to be policed by 100 inspectors and a system of fines.

The considerable constraints on individual initiative and business freedom created by the Davignon Plan (Mark II) had the whole-hearted and enthusiastic support of almost all the European Community's major steel firms. The Bresciani group were obliged to toe the line. Only the large efficient German firms, like Thyssen and Krupp, voiced their opposition to enforced cuts in output as a reward for having rationalised and streamlined production in the 1970s.

The gradual evolution of the European Community's steel policy – from informal 'voluntary' production quotas in 1977 to a full-scale compulsory system, armed with inspectors, reporting requirements and fines in 1980 – provides an object lesson in the dynamics of state control in capsule form. No businessman would normally support such direct interference with the daily running of his firm. Indeed, he starts by merely supporting vague notions of 'restraint', especially of foreign competitors, little suspecting that by doing so he is creating the sheltered conditions in which inefficiency flourishes, leading in due course to stronger and more coercive measures. Other members of society, who ultimately have to pay for the shelter thus provided, are similarly drawn into a situation which, had they foreseen it, would hardly have merited their support in the first place.

Once created, however, inefficiencies of such magnitude are extremely difficult to reverse. The European Community's stated objective is not only to cut steel production by about 14 per cent but also to cut jobs by 30/40 per cent from some 730 000 to between 500–600 000. But this part of the Community's steel plan has so far proved impossible to implement, because of the not unnatural resistance of the very firms for whose benefit the scheme was originally designed. And, behind the firms, stand their principal shareholders, the governments of Community member states. The latter have come to their rescue with all manner of soft loans, tax breaks, write-offs, grants, subsidies, loan-guarantees and state equity finance *in addition* to the Davignon Plan.

The reasons are not difficult to identify. First and foremost, the steel industry happens to be a very large employer in areas of already high regional unemployment; and democratically elected governments are afraid to let 'rationalisation' proceed either under pressure of market forces or under the tender guidance of the Commission of the European Community. Secondly, and probably spuriously, governments justify protection and inefficiency in such a 'basic' and 'strategic' sector as steel in terms of national defence. But if one needs a steel industry to wage war, would it not be better if it were efficient? Can one, in any case, speak plausibly of national defence considerations in the steel sector when one imports over 80 per cent of one's oil requirements? Is oil not a 'basic' or 'strategic' sector?

As a result of this mixture of political considerations, the European Community's guidelines for aid to the steel industry have remained safely in the zone of wishful thinking. They state that:

(i) aids should not be accorded for the sole purpose of preserving existing structures;

(ii) aids for modernising, rationalising or restructuring the industry should not lead to increases in capacity in sectors or sub-sectors in which there is manifest over-capacity;

(iii) aids to rescue a steel undertaking so as to enable an orderly adaptation to the new market situation should be of strictly limited duration and should take account of the structural modifications that are required; and

(iv) the form and intensity of aids should always be appropriate to their objectives – the problems the aids are intended to solve.[10]

Even more unrealistic is the hope that diverse national aid schemes might one day be superseded by a Community-wide restructuring plan.[11] The whole issue has by now become far too sensitive and problematic for member states to risk 'interference' from Brussels. As a result, the Davignon Plan contains all the elements of a negative industrial policy – cartelisation, protection, higher prices – without any of the redeeming features of a positive plan for structural reform.

There are other weak points in the Davignon Plan. Eight are discussed here.

1. By raising steel prices, it penalises steel users who may lose competitiveness as a result: this is a particular instance of the difficulties inherent in micro-economic industrial policies. Since all markets are inter-connected, sometimes obviously (as, for instance, steel and automobiles) and sometimes

mysteriously, but always unpredictably in quantitative terms, tinkering with one sector will have substantial, inevitable and frequently surprising effects in other areas. Since the European Community unquestionably exports far more steel embodied in its manufactured goods than it imports in this form, the Community's steel producers are (or should be) directly concerned with the preservation of competitiveness in the manufactured goods sector. Yet this competitiveness is directly reduced by higher steel prices. Protection against imports of manufactures containing steel is no answer because this will not restore export markets. It would therefore have been more prudent, from the point of view of the Community industry as a whole, to have let steel prices sink and to have offered steel producers subsidies which corresponded to the value collectively placed on the military/strategic and socio/political objectives served by them, along the lines of the French state enterprise contracts discussed in Chapter 3. Direct subsidisation, however, has been expressly rejected by the Commission as being 'no basis for policy' because of 'the enormous cost'.[12] This position ignores the infinitely larger indirect costs of high steel prices for the rest of the economy.

2. The Davignon Plan is caught in a contradiction between ends and means. The steel cartel of the European Community can only work if competition is suppressed. But if competition goes, so does the incentive to restructure and regain efficiency. Even more frustrating, competition may break out where it was supposed to be suppressed, but be successfully restricted in an area where it was supposed to flourish. This appears to have happened to Eurofer, whose members continued to flout the Davignon guidelines (total steel production rose in 1978), but operated 'secret Eurofer agreements for limiting cross-border steel sales between EEC members'.[13] Surely it cannot have been the Commission's intention to restrict intra-Community trade in this fashion!

3. The protection, cartelisation and subsidisation of the European Community's steel industry may provoke direct retaliation in which the Community can only be the net loser, since even its visible steel balance is in a comfortable surplus, not to speak of its 'invisible' trade balance.

4. Far more dangerous to the European Community's

Table 4.4

Asymmetry in the European Community's Trading Relationships, 1978

| | Trading partners' dependence on the Community (% of their total exports going to the Community) % | Community dependence on its respective trading partners (% of Community exports going to them) | |
		(a) including intra-Community trade %	(b) excluding intra-Community trade %
United States	22.3	6.5	11.5
Japan	10.7	1.0	1.9
EFTA	46.0	11.3	23.5
Non-oil exporting LDCs	25.7	9.1	18.9
India	20.0	0.4	0.8

Source: *International Trade 1978–79* (Geneva: GATT Secretariat, 1979).

industry as a whole would be retaliation involving manufactured products other than steel. This danger is often
underestimated because of the sheer size of the Community
taken collectively, relative to most of its trading partners, taken
individually. Thus India, for instance, relies on the Community
market for 20 per cent of her exports, while taking only 0.8 per
cent of the Community's exports in return.

Because of this asymmetry (highlighted in Table 4.4) the
European Community's trade ministers might be tempted to
think that any trade war would be infinitely more harmful to
others than to their own countries and that therefore no
country would be silly enough to start one. But a remarkable
example of threatened retaliation has recently cast doubt on
this comfortable illusion. Thus, Indonesia, in October 1980
threatened to cancel contracts for a methanol plant, oil refining
equipment, passenger aircraft, radar communications
equipment, 60 British Leyland double-decker buses and some
steel bailey bridges if the United Kingdom persisted in blocking

Indonesia's textile exports by means of emergency quotas imposed in conformity with the Community's bilateral agreement under the Multi-fibre Arrangement (MFA).[14]

The conflict, as yet unresolved at the time of writing, nicely underlines in clear political terms the point made under point 1 above, namely that all markets are interconnected and to protect one sector implies penalising others. The latent conflict between the export sector and the import-competing sector has, for once, been forced out into the open: are British jobs to be saved in textiles or in radar communications equipment?

5. Besides the not-so-theoretical danger of retaliation, the European Community will suffer from 'trade displacement'; that is, the indirect effects of limiting its trade partners' exports. These countries are good customers of the Community for all sorts of products. South Korea has become a large capital-goods importer. The very limitation of these countries' exports of steel, textiles and shoes to the Community reduces their demand for imports of more sophisticated products from the Community. The subtle 'trade displacement' effects of limiting developing countries' imports into the Community are potentially far more harmful than the obvious, but usually exaggerated, danger of retaliation.

6. Foreign steel producers, whose products can no longer enter the European Community freely, are not likely to sit back and do nothing. They will either export more steel to other countries, which, if they are steel producers, will soon erect barriers to imports themselves; or, as the available markets are slowly closed to their existing exports, they will look around for something else to make – something slightly higher up the evolutionary ladder of industrialisation. Import restrictions on simple products with low value-added may therefore result in competition re-appearing somewhere else. Fears for instance have been expressed by the British forgers' association that the Community's restriction on steel imports 'is leading to overseas producers moving into semi-manufacturing to maintain their exports'.[15] Japan offers an example from the recent past of how quickly a country can alter its export structure to avoid trade restrictions. In the 1950s Japan exported cotton textiles, toys and ceramics to Western Europe and North America. As these

were progressively restricted, Japan moved on to ships, steel, cameras, radios and television sets. These, too, became subject to orderly marketing arrangements in many countries, and Japan shifted yet once more, this time into electronics, computers and non-polluting, fuel-efficient automobiles.

This pattern of development would have occurred anyway, but the protectionist response of other developed countries at each stage in the process undoubtedly provided a considerable incentive to move ahead as fast as possible. Does the Community really want to accelerate the problem of structural adjustment for itself by providing good reasons for rapidly developing countries to diversify their exports and climb faster up the ladder of development? Protecting the Community's basic steel industry will have consequences going far beyond saving apparent jobs and keeping an industry on its feet for military and social reasons. It is in the process of creating far more problems than it is supposed to solve.

7. Although trade restrictions can prevent imports from penetrating home markets, nothing can protect the European Community's steel producers from competition in overseas markets. The Community's visible steel exports, it will be recalled, run at well over *twice* the value of steel imports, while the invisible steel surplus is probably even higher. It is likely to decline drastically for two reasons. First the Community and American 'trigger price' mechanisms and import restraints will divert steel away from them and into third-country markets. The Community's own exports of steel will therefore encounter fiercer competition than ever. Furthermore, steel prices will fall in countries which do not attempt to protect themselves, thus giving their steel-using manufacturing industries a substantial advantage, further undermining the competitive position of the Community's steel-using manufactures, both at home and abroad.

8. Finally, although it looks as though the steel industry's plight is due to imports, its root cause lies more in technological change and the increased cost of energy. Older energy-intensive plants are not competitive and newer plants need fewer people to operate them. The countries of the European Community are as capable as any others in the world of producing steel

efficiently by using the latest technologies. Sooner or later an enterprising firm will do so. What will the others do then? Ask for the reintroduction of intra-Community tariffs or for a reinforcement of the cartel? Ultimately, neither the governments of member countries nor the Commission can protect an industry from technological change and relative price shifts, except at great cost.

Each one of the drawbacks to the Davignon Plan is worthy of serious consideration. Together they represent a strong case for a change of policy. Yet such is the level of public debate on the issue that at the very most only the most obvious costs are discussed (such as the impact on the competitiveness of steel-using industries) and then only to be dismissed.

Future Shape of the Industry

In West Germany, the restructuring of the steel industry will probably take the form of yet more mergers, with due elimination of surplus capacity, and an efficient slimmed-down steel industry will doubtless emerge in the 1980s without much direct government help. In France, the government introduced a rescue programme in 1977, costing 12 000 million francs, and aimed to reduce the workforce by 16 000 by the end of 1979.[16] By September 1978 France's eight steel producers had made accumulated losses amounting to 40 000 million francs (about $8000 million) and the government came to their rescue by converting part of their losses into state equity shareholding and covering the remainder with loans and guarantees. This was nationalisation in all but name. In Belgium, the state has come to the help of ailing steel firms, Cockerill, Hainaut-Sambre and Thy-Marcinelle-et-Monceau, by providing stop-gap finance and in exchange taking shares in the companies. Banks are also being asked to extend credit lines by 20 per cent and to cut the interest on them by 2 points.[17] Willy Claes, as Minister of Economics, predicted that the state would have a majority interest in Cockerill by 1982.[18] Clearly more mergers and possibly nationalisations are on the cards for the Belgian steel industry.

In Italy, the state-owned Italsider and Finsider groups are enormous lossmakers for IRI and stand in sharp, and embarrassing, contrast to the efficiency and profitability of the small independent steel producers in the north. It is well understood that in Italy it is virtually out of the question to shut down inefficient state-owned plant, so it was a considerable victory for the Commission of the European Community when it stopped the construction of a huge new steel complex at Gioia Tauro in Calabria. The *Financial Times* reported that 'the EEC intervention in fact was welcomed by the Italian authorities who could not see how they could get out of the steel proposal.'[19] Quite why stopping the construction of a brand-new and presumably reasonably efficient steel plant to replace out-dated facilities elsewhere should be considered such an achievement is difficult to see. In fact steel producers elsewhere (possibly even within the same giant firm) were probably fearful of the potential com-petition and succeeded in scotching the project. There are, as always, arguments on both sides. The principal one against the Gioria Tauro project was the massive state aid with which it was being built and which caused 'private' steel producers in other Community countries to complain about unfair competition: a case of the pot calling the kettle black?

In Britain the steel industry has been a political football since World War II. First it was nationalised, then sold back to private interests, then nationalised again – just in time for the worst steel recession in post-war history. In 1975, the BSC published the 'Beswick Review' of the industry, in which a number of plants were named for closure and it was proposed to reduce the workforce by 18 000 (to 190 000) by 1980. The cost of modernisation, restructuring and moving slowly towards this target has proved very high. BSC's losses have been running at between £300–£400 million a year for several years and its outstanding level of debt by 1980 will probably be over £5000 million. Not even the Labour Government of James Callaghan, devoted to the workers' cause, could justify continued subsidies at such a rate and BSC in fact closed down several obsolete plants, dismissing 15 000 people in 1977–78 and was prepared to continue. The Conservative Government of Mrs Thatcher ac-celerated the process by announcing that it expected BSC to break even by March 1980. In December 1979 the Corporation stated that it intended to reduce its labour force from 182 000 to 130 000 – a total of 52 000 jobs.[20] The political obstacles that such an uncompromis-ing policy could expect to encounter rapidly materialised, in the form a long and widely-supported strike, which ended with a small increase in wages but no deviation from rationalisation. It emphasised the need for finding practical ways of defusing resistance to change without stopping the process of change itself.

Looking ahead it seems as though most of the European Community steel-making capacity will soon be owned by the state, with the possible exception of West Germany. It constitutes a very good example of how industrial policy, starting out with the best of job-preserving intentions, gets caught up in its own dynamic. After a while, there seems to be no alternative except more government intervention, and certainly none that is 'politically acceptable'. From the point of nationalisation, however, there are two possible ways to go: either to run the operation as a public utility, whose purpose is principally to provide jobs (at a high cost) in areas of high unemployment, or to run it on commercial lines, in which case it should be sold back to private interests after the structural change has taken place. What is certain is that the Community will continue to produce steel and could do so competitively. Although it is fashionable to speak about the need for Western Europe to concentrate on 'knowledge-intensive' goods, this does not mean that the crude steel, textiles or clothing industries have to disappear. There is presumably a place for their more efficient segments in the new international division of labour, providing they accept the need to change. The problem is the size of the change. The Commission has proposed a reduction of employment in steel from 750 000 to 500 000. What will probably be needed is a drop to 300 000. To redeploy half a million people in a low-growth period is a frightening prospect, but one which has to be faced because the alternative is even worse: the re-deployment of many more people not only in the steel-using sectors but also in many quite unrelated sectors. Also, given that some degree of structural unemployment is unavoidable, it is surely easier to bear if one knows that the economy is becoming more efficient rather than less, since the prospects for future growth and employment will be better.

Shipbuilding: 'Orderly Marketing' Protection and Subsidies

The problems of the European Community's steel industry can, in part, be traced back to the troubles of the shipbuilding industry which is, in normal times, a large consumer of steel. But shipyards can be protected from foreign competition even less than the Community's steel mills. At least 30 per cent of the value of Community ship production is exported (that is, registered outside the Community). Shipyards in the Community can therefore only survive if they are competitive internationally. The Association of West European Shipbuilders (AWES) does not believe that this is an impossible objective: 'Price gaps between European and Far East yards existed, but were not as great as was sometimes suggested. The challenge to restore competitive prices was fully accepted by European builders.'[21]

The problem at present is sheer over-capacity due to a drastic reduction in the demand for ships, especially tankers, since the oil crisis which broke in 1973. The Commission of the European Community has been working on the problem for some years, trying to reduce the intensity of member states' aids in order to prevent senseless over-subsidisation, and also trying to persuade the Japanese to accept 'voluntary' restraints. In 1977, the Japanese agreed to raise their prices by 5 per cent and, coupled with a rising yen and various subsidies to shipowners in the Community this meant that the thirteen members of AWES were able to build slightly more than Japanese yards in terms of 'compensated tonnes' in 1977 and their order books for 1978 were considerably fuller (8.6 million tonnes as compared with 5.5 million tonnes for Japan).

This combination of 'orderly marketing' protection and state subsidisation provides the European Community's shipyards with what is intended to be a temporary breathing space, during which they are supposed to restructure. According to the Commission, the Community's shipbuilding industry will have to cut capacity by 46 per cent and its workforce by 50 000 people if it is to regain competitiveness.[22]

There is once more, however, a wide gap between what one knows must be done and what actually happens. Individual member states' restructuring plans are in most cases long over-due, there is little evidence of radical cuts in capacity, and the Commission has been unable to prevent a steady escalation in the level of assistance.

In fact, if one goes back to 1972, the year of the second directive on shipping, one can read nostalgically that subsidies must not exceed 5 per cent of the ex-yards price of newly-built ships. Furthermore, this ceiling was to be degressive over the three-year life-span of the directive. In 1975, significantly, the third directive mentioned no subsidy ceiling. By 1977 Italy, France and the United Kingdom were offering price subsidies of between 20 and 30 per cent of the end cost and by the time the Commission issued its fourth directive, in December 1978, one was not surprised to see that member states were being held to aid ceilings of 30 per cent. These, as the Commission itself deplored,[23] constituted a virtual 100 per cent subsidy on the value added to intermediate goods, since shipbuilding is essentially assembly work. This implies, of course, that the pre-subsidy contribution of shipbuilding to GNP is equal or close to zero in the United Kingdom, France and Italy.

In view of the steady escalation of aid over time since 1972, can one really still speak of 'temporary' breathing spaces? Far from being degressive, shipping aids have progressed over time. As has already been argued elsewhere, this is not surprising: subsidies discourage efficiency and in turn create the need for more subsidies in the future. What *is* surprising is that the process is not checked by those who are elected to govern in the general interests of their country.

Chemicals: Counter-cyclical Measures

Chemicals, like steel, are an essential industrial building block. Demand for them, as for steel, is a derived demand – that is, it is governed by the demand for its sometimes remote end-products. Growth in the industry does not only depend on the ingenuity and skill of the firms directly involved in chemical manufacture, but on the success or failure of a myriad of firms further down-stream in the chain of production.

In the past, the demand for chemicals grew between twice to three times as fast as GNP and the principal problem of the chemical industry was how to expand capacity fast enough to keep up with it. When an industry grows this fast, it is usually for one of two reasons: either it offers better or cheaper direct substitutes for existing products (synthetic fibres and chemical fertilisers are noteworthy examples), in which case it grows at the expense of traditional sectors which it partly or completely replaces; or it offers entirely new products (for example, detergents, drugs, insecticides) in which case markets will grow at the expense of all others, as consumers shift expenditure in their direction. The chemical industry was able to grow so spectacularly in the past because *both* these factors were present at the same time.

The question is whether the stagnation in demand for chemicals which began in the mid-1970s is a temporary lull, or whether this process of substitution and creativity has come to an abrupt end. If so, the chemical industry will have to be content with an average growth in demand.

It may seem paradoxical that an industry which exports $1.40 worth of chemicals for every $1 worth of imports, and which has not experienced an actual drop in demand, should find itself in a critical position. Serious over-capacity in the European Community's chemical industry can be traced back to an unfortunate conjunction of circumstances which greatly magnified the effects of the slowdown in growth in the world economy.

First, economies of scale are important, so investment tends to be 'lumpy' (that is, cannot be fractioned over time). This was no problem in the past because as demand grew at between 10 and 15 per cent a year capacity had to double every five to seven years. Also, new investments take at least three years to complete because of the sheer size and complexity of a modern chemical plant. These three factors together meant that the investments to increase capacity in the 1970–73 boom years, in anticipation of future growth at the same rate as in the past, came on-stream in 1975–78 when the demand was not there. In fact, it had hardly grown at all, with the result that the European Community's chemical industry by 1978 had 20 to 40 per cent excess capacity in some important sectors.

These problems are exacerbated by the fact that investments in some countries – notably fibres in Italy and petro-chemicals in Britain – have gone ahead in spite of the 'recession' as part of their governments' industrial policy: building chemical plants provides many jobs over several years and when the 'recession' comes to an end, the plant is there to satisfy demand – the ideal counter-cyclical measure!

Trade Picture for Chemicals

Unlike steel or textiles, the European Community's chemical industry does not have to worry about competition from low-wage countries. It is a capital-intensive and technology-intensive industry *par excellence*. It does have to worry, however, about competition from areas which have a comparative advantage in the production of chemical raw materials, especially petroleum. Petroleum-producing countries have both the ambition to raise the value-added content of their exports and the financial resources to invest in such projects. This situation is full of implications for Community chemical producers. Should they supply the technology, capital equipment and engineering know-how which investing countries lack, thus knowingly building up competition for the future?

They have, in fact, already gone through one such cycle in Eastern Europe. In the heyday of rapid expansion in the latter 1960s, chemical producers fell over themselves to sell plants to Eastern Europe, in payment for which they agreed to 'buy back' part of the future production. This capacity came on-stream in the mid-1970s at just the wrong time. For instance, polyethylene from two Russian plants built by the West German state-owned Salzgitter began entering the German market at the end of 1977, at a time when there was already 50 per cent over-capacity in the industry. Nor is this all. Many more buy-back agreements will only begin to have an effect in the 1980s. Some examples include: 250 000 tons of ammonia a year as from 1981 (Montedison), 300 000 tons of methanol a year as from 1981 (ICI, Klöckner), benzine and petro-chemicals at $500 million (Technip, France), ammonia, methanol and xylenes worth $1100 million (Rhône-Poulenc).[24] With demand stagnant these buy-back agreements serve to depress already weak prices. Much the same thing is happening in the Middle East, although chemical firms are taking ready cash, instead of payment in kind, for their exports of plants. This detail does not alter the fact that when these plants actually start producing they will perhaps be serving an already crowded market. In addition, the European Community's chemical producers have had to contend with competition from, of all countries, the United States, stemming from allegedly lower prices for petroleum-based feed-stocks than are current in the Community.

All of this does not add up to a case for an industrial policy in chemicals. Nor is there one yet. But it is perhaps noteworthy that Table 3.3 above shows that the chemical industry quite clearly outstrips all others in terms of the number of instances of special *ad hoc* government support it managed to attract in 1977 and 1978 and the man-made fibre end of the industry even managed to catch the eye of Viscount Davignon (see below). In fact, there is little cause for alarm:

(a) The European Community's trade surplus in chemicals rose from $6780 million in 1973 to $15 530 million in 1978; although part of this is due to relative price increases in the sector, and to inflation, it still constitutes one of the Community's largest net export sectors.

(b) The industry is capital intensive and thus rationalisation, if needed, will not pose insuperable social problems; there is therefore no reason why it should lose competitiveness in the future.

(c) Demand for its products will grow rapidly in all developing countries. World-wide there is no reason to believe that excess capacity will be a chronic problem.

(d) On the question of whether producers in developed countries should sell their know-how if it means creating competition for the future. The answer is that they have no choice. If company A refuses, company B or C will agree to do it. Again, the only formula for long-term survival is not to resist change, but to move with it.

(e) Most chemical firms and their shareholders can look back on thirty years of uninterrupted growth. Admittedly, it is easier to adapt to positive than to negative change, but this industry, more than most, is used to having to change its plans and adapt them to the market. It is therefore better armed than some to cope with the down-side.

(f) Finally, the fact that the Commission of the European Community negotiated a 35 per cent tariff cut on chemicals in the Tokyo Round negotiations[25] suggests that the long-term strength of the Community's chemical industry is not really in serious doubt.

Plastics

Of all the micro-sectors of the chemical industry, fibres and plastics have been the worst hit. Producers of plastics have gone to the European Community for help, some of them doubtless hoping for a combination of import restrictions and an agreement between producers to cut capacity, but they have had to content themselves with less.

The Commission of the European Community agreed in May 1978[26] to conduct a factual survey of plastic capacity in Western Europe, future expansion plans, expected levels of demand, imports and exports and to centralise information on buy-back agreements. The survey covered only the major commodity plastics – low-density and high-density polyethylene, polypropylene, PVC and polystyrene – which have been suffering most from over-capacity and sudden surges of imports from Eastern Europe under buy-back arrangements. One purpose the study served was to shed light on the contention of the European Community's chemical firms that some producers, notably in Eastern Europe and in Italy, are not required to earn a full market return on investment, but are happy if they can service their debt with something to spare, while firms subject to normal market constraints have to earn enough to repay their debts, to re-invest and to keep their shareholders happy. According to them it is very difficult to compete with firms which are required to meet lower standards of profitability.

The Commission of the European Community announced in April 1979 that as far as imports from Comecon are concerned, and especially plastics, it will no longer judge dumping cases on the basis of whether goods have been exported below the exporters' costs (which are deemed to be spurious in the case of Comecon), but according to whether they have entered the Community at below 'normal value' – that is, at below the cost of an 'efficient West European producer'.[27] This system of judging whether dumping has occurred or not will be much easier to apply than the former one. It is illegal in terms of the GATT and the new customs valuation code,[28] but since few members of Comecon are members of the GATT, this is no problem. It in fact confronts the planning price fiction with the equally arbitrary notion of 'normal value' and constitutes a genteel form of retaliation against the abuse of state trading practices.

For the moment there does not seem to be much support for a 'crisis cartel' in plastics to plan cuts in capacity and to share them out 'equitably'. Even the European Community's Commission is reported 'to be extremely reluctant to allow manufacturers to move towards a cartel arrangement',[29] while Viscount Davignon 'has also pointed out to the industry that it is to blame for many of its present difficulties'.[30]

The industry itself is divided. The very same firms which have agreed to planned cuts in capacity in the fibres sector (see below) are reluctant to do the same for plastics. While the weaker Italian, French and Dutch firms are pressing for such a plan, the stronger West German and British firms are reluctant to have their wings clipped. According to British industrial leaders, the answer is for older, less efficient plants to be closed and for less efficient producers to get out of the market; protection would only make the European Community's industry uncompetitive in world markets.[31] What clearer statement in favour of market-induced structural change and the virtues of efficiency could there be?

This being so, the outside observer may be forgiven for asking why these arguments did not apply with equal strength to the fibre sector where a 'crisis cartel' was arranged. The answer seems to have been that plastics were less of a problem than fibres. They commanded a much larger market, were more competitive, suffered little from imports, and had better long-term growth prospects. A small increase in prices would make them healthy again. Fibres, on the other hand, were linked to the European Community's textile industry, and were therefore condemned to a future of slow or even nil growth. In these circumstances, prudence alone suggested that an orderly market-sharing arrangement would be preferable (at least for the fibre industry) to an unseemly scramble for customers (who would be the only beneficiaries of the free-for-all).

In short, one reaches the same conclusion as did Adam Smith two centuries ago, namely that one cannot expect large firms to be unwavering supporters of the market system: they will (not unnaturally) uphold it or not, according to the interest of the day, the place and the product.

Textiles and Clothing

Along with steel, the most troubled sector of European industry is undoubtedly textiles. The troubles start right at the start of the chain of production with the man-made fibre industry and continue right down to zips and T-shirts.

Fibres

Fibre producers in Western Europe have seen their share of world production decline from 31 per cent in 1970 to 22.5 per cent in 1977, according to figures supplied by Enka.[32] This has been attributed in large measure to the decline of the European Community's textile and clothing industry relative to that of developing countries and Eastern Europe and also to the expansion of fibre capacity in these countries to serve local demand. Much of this fibre capacity in developing countries has been created with the help of West European, American and Japanese chemical firms, which should do so since they have the technology, know-how and capital. But they cannot expect to sell plant and technology, or experience the risks and profits of direct investment, *and* export the same goods as well. This would be having one's cake and eating it too.

Nevertheless, the man-made fibre industry, after years of spectacular growth was apparently taken by surprise. It saw its export markets gradually disappearing and its domestic market shrinking rapidly as imports took ever larger shares, not only of basic fibre requirements, but also of semi-finished and finished goods, such as clothing and household furnishings. But this was not all. It noted with dismay the way the Italian Government, in blind disregard of market conditions and the exhortations of the Commission of the European Community, poured money into expanding synthetic fibre capacity – precisely the sector which has notched up the most gigantic losses for IRI.

The industry therefore went to the Commission of the European Community with its troubles and, under the auspices of the Directorate-General for Industrial Affairs and with the help of Viscount Davignon, the Community's eleven principal fibre producers[33] agreed in the summer of 1978 on a plan to share out the existing market according to the pattern of deliveries in 1976. Any loss in demand would be shared equally, as well as any growth, an exception being made for Italy on the grounds that because she was a late starter she had a 'right' to a larger share in the Community's man-made fibre production.[34]

This agreement lay beyond the law as laid down in Article 85 of the Treaty of Rome. It could not be justified in terms of any of the escape clauses provided. It did not improve the production or distribution of goods. Nor did it promote technical or economic progress. It was just an old-fashioned market-sharing agreement and as such needed special dispensation from Brussels. This could only be provided by the Council of Ministers, acting unanimously, and here the differences in member states' attitudes to industrial policy began to surface. While the French, British and Italian governments supported the fibre agreement, the West German Government refused to endorse it. Indeed, it presented definite drawbacks:

(a) It created a precedent and from then on any industry suffering from the vicissitudes of the market or government policy or the unpleasant consequences of its own past decisions could run to Brussels for permission to form a private cartel in the public interest.

(b) Cooperation in one segment of the chemical industry (that is, fibres) could spill over, via the 'group effect', into other segments of the industry, already one of the most concentrated in the European Community.

(c) Once formed, even if there were a time limit on the agreement, it might prove difficult to disband such a cartel once the crisis was over. Market sharing would become even more of a habit than it already was and the competitive spirit might die. If so, the industry would cease to be internationally competitive, and would soon need permanent protection.

(d) The cartel was not accompanied by a logical plan to eliminate the least efficient plants in the fibre industry. Rather, by making each firm 'share' the burden of cutting over-capacity 'fairly', the most efficient firms would have had to do most of the cutting.

In the event the fibre cartel was never officially approved, but nor was it prosecuted. Are we to believe that it never went into operation and that European fibre producers are at present competing fiercely with each other? As in the case of steel, the fibre cartel was accompanied by import restrictions – indeed, without them, the cartel would have failed immediately. These in any case have survived.

Trade Picture for Textiles

In July 1977, France introduced unilateral quotas on T-shirts and other particularly fast-selling items, in an eleventh-hour attempt to save, *inter alia*, the Boussac textile conglomerate. The Commission of the European Community faced the unenviable choice of *either* taking France to the European Court for breach of the common external commercial policy *or* generalising the quota restrictions. It chose the latter. In the ensuing periods it negotiated much stricter quota restrictions on developing-country (LDC) products in the framework of the renewal of the Multi-fibre Arrangement (MFA).[35] The latter, signed in 1973 for four years, coming into force in 1974, was up for renewal. It was designed to limit the growth of textile exports from developing to developed countries to a maximum 6 per cent a year, but was loosely applied with the result that imports of many individual items grew faster.

This rate of growth proved too rapid for the European Community's ailing textile mills and clothing factories and the bilateral quotas, negotiated under a protocol to the renewed MFA of 1978, came into force for five years and virtually stabilised trade at

1976 levels.[36] This 'breathing space' was supposed to be used by the industry to cut back on surplus capacity, eliminate its old and inefficient plant, and emerge rejuvenated in the early 1980s. The industry was soon protesting that it needed more time.

It is useful to make a clear distinction between the yarn and fabric manufacturers, on the one hand, and the clothing producers, on the other. Although their destinies are linked, they are very different. The first sector is capital-intensive, technology-intensive and skill-intensive and is concentrated into a few large firms, some of which are integrated backwards into the chemical sector. The clothing sector is labour-intensive and is much more fragmented. There is little integration between the two sectors because the mix of skills and factors is so different for each. Their interests, moreover, do not always coincide. While it is in the interest of the large textile mills to have a captive local domestic clothing sector, it is in the interests of the latter to be able to buy cloth from all over the world. In the present crisis, protection has been given to both sectors. Since the second sector is no longer free to buy as many cheap textiles from the Far East as it desires, this comprehensive system of protection works in favour of the textile and fibre producers, but its long-term usefulness to the clothing industry is doubtful.

Does the plight of the fibre and textile industry merit such discrimination in its favour?

The European Community's trade in yarns and fabrics is in fact in surplus. A very slight deterioration in the ratio of exports to imports is discernible, falling from 1.23 in 1972 to 1.10 in 1978, but is hardly of crisis proportions (see Table 4.5). This confirms that the up-stream end of the Community textile industry remains basically competitive; however, it is alarmed at the loss of competitiveness of its principal customer, the Community clothing industry. It has therefore added its own weight to clothing's pleas for protection. One might even venture to guess that the lobbying powers of the dispersed clothing industry have been strengthened and amplified by the support of the far more concentrated and better organised fibre and textile sector. But, as pointed out above, the latter is an ally of doubtful value for the clothing industry. When the clothing industry was in trouble, ICI announced an increase of 13–14 per cent in the price of most fibres and yarns, effective from 1 July 1978.[37]

The European Community's import restrictions reflect its attempts to please both parties. Thus the import quota on man-made fibres, yarns and fabrics from developing countries is only 2.6 per cent of

Table 4.5

Ratio of the European Community's Exports to Imports in Textiles compared with EFTA's Position, 1972–78

	European Community.	EFTA
1972	1.23	0.81
1973	1.22	0.82
1974	1.22	0.80
1975	1.17	0.80
1976	1.12	0.80
1977	1.12	0.75
1978	1.10	0.91

Source: *International Trade 1978–79* (Geneva: GATT Secretariat, 1979).

Community production. It is therefore of considerable benefit to local producers of such products. On the other hand, the import quota on cotton yarns and fabrics is much larger and amounts to 30 per cent of Community production. This is therefore of no value to producers but of considerable benefit to users in the clothing industry (see Table 4.6).

Future Prospects

Textile production is capable of being increasingly automated; and

Table 4.6

Ratio of Quotas to Domestic Production of Textiles in the European Community, 1977

European Community	Cotton (tonnes)	Man-made (tonnes)
Domestic production	832 000	1 413 000
Quotas	251 263	37 322
Ratio of quotas to domestic produce	30%	2.6%

Sources: *Journal Officiel des Communautés Européennes*, Brussels, no. L357, 31 December 1977, for the quotas and *Statistiques des base*, Commission of the European Community, 1977, for production figures. The countries to which the quotas apply are Brazil, Colombia, Egypt, Hong Kong, India, Malaysia, Mexico, Pakistan, Peru, Rumania, Singapore, South Korea, Thailand and Yugoslavia.

labour costs can be reduced to a negligible fraction, relative to capital, material inputs and design costs. The European Community can remain efficient in this section of the industry providing governments are prepared to risk redundancies and allow change. There are signs that they are prepared to do so. In the United Kingdom for instance, Carrington Viyella in 1978 closed two old spinning mills and opened a new one with a threefold improvement in output.[38] In France, in the same year, the Boussac empire had been allowed to go into receivership.[39] In the Netherlands eight loss-making spinning mills were forced to merge by the state, which then took a 49 per cent share in the new firm. It was explained that they shed about 1250 of their 2700 workforce.[40] In West Germany most of the labour-intensive stages of textile manufacture have been displaced eastwards.

While the European Community will continue to be a large (and, one hopes, efficient) fibre/fabric producer, the size of this industry relative to all others will at best remain stationary, or diminish, because the income-elasticity of demand for clothing is roughly unity (Europeans spend around a steady 5 per cent of GNP on clothing). In the meantime, competitive pressure will mount, both in the Community and in third markets. Unless the Community textile industry can meet this competition successfully, especially abroad, its relative size must shrink.

Table 4.7

Ratio of Exports to Imports in Clothing in the European Community compared with EFTA's Position, 1972–78

	European Community	EFTA
1972	0.92	0.60
1973	0.84	0.75
1974	0.79	0.63
1975	0.76	0.58
1976	0.72	0.51
1977	0.76	0.41
1978	0.75	0.44

Source: *International Trade 1978–79* (Geneva: GATT Secretariat, 1979).

Clothing

The further down-stream in the textile industry one goes, however, the larger the problems become. The European Community's clothing industry has been on the sick list for years. It is highly fragmented and many firms owe their existence to government aid in one way or another. It has lost an estimated 500 000 people since 1973[41] and the ratio of exports to imports has deteriorated steadily as countries with abundant low-cost labour have begun supplying the market in substantial quantities (see Table 4.7).

The European Community's cotton and clothing industries have enjoyed a certain measure of protection since the early 1960s, first through the Long Term Arrangement of 1962 and then through the MFA,[42] but this has not proved enough to prevent the gradual deterioration of business conditions. Since January 1978, however, the Community's quota system has provided comprehensive protection right across the board, although the MFA comes up for negotiation in 1981. The agreements with developing countries which began in 1978 were designed to last four to five years, during which period clothing firms in the Community were expected to merge, specialise and shed yet more people. This they would have done even faster without the benefit of protective quotas, so their purpose is to buy time for the industry and, too, for governments, in view of the many firms and people involved.

The European Community's quota system divides products into six groups, the first of which contains the 'ultra-sensitive' products, where the rate of import-penetration is deemed to be 'very high'. The second group comprises 'sensitive' products, where the rate of import-penetration is somewhat lower, and so on down to the sixth group where the dangers are more potential than real, and where the purpose of the Community licensing system is said to be more statistical than protective. No growth at all has been foreseen up to 1982 for products in Groups I and II and only slow growth in Group III.

Individual quotas are fixed in volume terms (tonnes of fabric or pieces of clothing) for both the exporting country and specific member states of the European Community so that each member is sure to carry its 'share' of the 'burden' of imports. Developing countries help administer the system. Their customs authorities receive the appropriate number of Community import licences which

Table 4.8

Illustrative Selection of Textile Products Subject to Quotas in the European Community

Brief description	Quotas	Per person
Group I: (complete)		
Cotton yarn, not for retail sale	68 620 tonnes	260 gr.
Cotton fabric, bleached or unbleached	144 895 tonnes	553 gr.
Cotton fabric 'other' (i.e. dyed or patterned)	27 489 tonnes	104 gr.
Synthetic fabric woven, bleached or unbleached	19 476 tonnes	75 gr.
Synthetic fabric woven 'other' (i.e. dyed or patterned)	8 569 tonnes	33 gr.
Under-garments: shirts, T-shirts, etc.	113.8 million pieces	0.4 pieces
Jerseys, pullovers, jumpers of wool, cotton or man-made fibres	89 million pieces	0.3 pieces
Shorts, slacks, trousers	81 million pieces	0.3 pieces
Women's, girls' and infants' shirts and blouses	88 million pieces	0.3 pieces
Men's and boys' shirts	130 million pieces	0.5 pieces
Group II: (sample)		
Terry towelling	10 253 tonnes	39 gr.
Gloves and mittens	75 million pairs	0.3 pairs
Stockings and socks, other than tights	121 million pairs	0.4 pairs
Underpants	82 million pairs	0.3 pairs
Men's and boys' overcoats and rain coats	11 million pieces	0.04 pieces
Women's and girls' overcoats and rain coats	14.8 million pieces	0.05 pieces
Men's and boys' suits (woven)	4.8 million pieces	0.02 pieces
Men's and boys' jackets and blazers	10.6 million pieces	0.04 pieces
Handkerchiefs < 15 EUA/kg	17 million pieces	0.06 pieces
Bed linen	9 203 tonnes	35 gr.
Parkas, anoraks, jackets and so on	16 million pieces	0.06 pieces

Source: *Journal Officiel des Communautes Européennes*, Brussels, no. L357/10, 31 December 1977.

Note: Quotas on a per capita basis were derived from using the population of the European Community of nine member countries, namely 260 million people, as the denominator.

they deliver to their own exporters. The value of these licences, in view of their limited supply, is considerable. Who captures the quasi-rents? These are large and undoubtedly help to sweeten the pill of export restraints for some. Administrative problems at the Community end are also substantial. Spot checks are needed to discourage fraud. Origin certificates have to be attached to all shipments of textiles, even of Community origin, if trade deflection is to be prevented and the Community's internal quota system preserved.

The quota system involves 123 product groups. This may not sound much, but diligent perusal of the relevant issue of the European Community's *Official Journal* will convince one that it has left out nothing of importance. It would be tedious to enumerate them all, but a selection of items in Groups I and II ('ultra-sensitive' and 'sensitive') gives the flavour of the system (see Table 4.8). They read like a generous clothes list. Group III contains many fabrics, both natural and man-made. Group IV contains mainly knitted clothes, stockings and bathing suits. Group V seems to be aimed mainly at the leisure industry and limits imports of camping and sailing equipment. Group VI covers household furnishings.

Now that protection has been provided, clothing manufacturers are being encouraged to limit capacity. The knitwear producers notified an agreement to reduce over-capacity in women's tights, estimated at around 40 per cent, because of (i) the drastic change in fashions from mini-skirts to jeans and (ii) a rapid expansion of Italian production.[43] The story of the Bresciani mini-steel mills is indeed likely to be repeated, since Italian tights production is not in the hands of large concentrated firms, but is literally farmed out. Peasants in northern Italy have reportedly sold their cows and installed knitting machines in their stables instead, because subsidised Italian machinery manufacturers built for stock during the recession and then dumped quantities of knitting machines on the market. This is an apt illustration of how subsidies in one sector (in this case the knitting machinery sector) can cause considerable damage to another sector (in this case the tights market): the problem is shifted to other shoulders, but is not solved.

Will the knitwear producers' agreement to reduce capacity and specialise be repeated in other segments of the market? Such agreements do not necessarily fall foul of Article 85 of the Treaty of Rome, which provides for agreements between firms which 'contribute to the improvement of the production or distribution of goods'. Specialisation agreements, especially between small firms, would probably pass muster. Because of the fragmented nature of the industry, its progressive cartelisation is, paradoxically, likely to be permitted. An alternative would be to apply Article 85 strictly and allow specialisation and rationalisation to occur in a 'disorderly' fashion.

Giving the European Community's formula of protection-cum-cartelisation the benefit of the doubt, and assuming that it will be disbanded in the early 1980s, is there any hope for the long-term survival of an efficient and competitive clothing industry in the Community? There are two reasons for optimism.

First, the accession of Greece, Portugal and Spain to the European Community should not be viewed as a threat, but positively as a way to force clothing industries in the north to face reality. Both the northern and southern countries of the Community would gain from mutual specialisation, which could be encouraged by Brussels, which would help a leaner Community industry to face competition from the Far East in the mid-1980s with confidence. This will only happen, however, if it is made quite clear that protection will come to an end on time.

Secondly, laser and micro-processor technologies appear to have found useful applications in clothing manufacture. Lasers are used to cut through many thicknesses of cloth hyperaccurately. Computers calculate how to cut so as to reduce waste to a minimum. Sewing machines now have memories and can 'learn' to repeat up to 50 consecutive operations. The operator simply guides the cloth and one wonders how long it will take for the human operator to be replaced by a robot prepared to work 24 hours a day.

Clearly, even in a labour-intensive industry like clothing, the substitution of labour by capital is feasible – although costly. Industrialists in the European Community must decide whether this would constitute a sensible investment, but the only way to ensure that the socially optimal amount of labour-saving investment is actually undertaken would be to expose the industry to free trade with the most efficient, lowest-cost producers in the world. As it is, there is a risk that as a result of exhortation, subsidisation and distortion of market signals, developed countries may over-invest in labour-saving innovations in the clothing sector. This is not only wasteful of (scarce) innovative talent. It does not solve the political problem of unemployment, for it matters little to the unemployed sewing-machine operator whether she loses her job because of imports or because a machine can now do her work.

Conclusions

Each industry discussed here suffers from a different problem. Chemicals and plastics, for instance, suffer mainly from a cyclical fall in demand and hence from temporary over-capacity. Their troubles will disappear as the economy begins to expand, but they may never experience again the intoxicating rates of growth of yesteryear. Man-made fibres, on the other hand, face (in addition to cyclical troubles) a long-term structural decline in the rate of growth, compared with the past. Growth at the expense of natural fibres has come to an abrupt halt and the prospects for technological change are presumably no longer what they were. Shipyards face a modest cyclical drop in demand, since their fortunes are linked to those of world trade in general, which in turn is linked to the recession. World trade, however, has tended to be more buoyant than many national economies, because business cycles do not usually coincide (1974–76 was an exception in this respect) and thus most of the shipyards' problems must be structural: fierce international competition, greater productivity of ships, lighter cargoes due to pressure from developing countries to do more processing locally and to the progressive miniaturisation of everything else, competition from air cargo, and so forth. This industry clearly cannot put off substantial cut-backs much longer. Finally, steel faces both cyclical and structural problems, the latter consisting mainly of international competitive pressure which, in the absence of political and social problems, would probably have resulted in the spontaneous adoption of the most cost-efficient production techniques by private steel-makers by now. As it is, the change implies an enormous reduction in the work force (not from 750 000 to 500 000 as suggested by the Commission of the European Community, but probably to as little as 250 000, if other reports are to be believed[44]). No government in the Community is prepared to contemplate it, at least not in its own political life-span. The answer everywhere has been to slow the process down as much as possible. Even if the Community steel industry succeeds in shedding 25 000 people a year, which is considerable, it will still take twenty years to regain its international competitiveness. Can the Community wait that long? Are there any alternatives?

NOTES

1. *Yearbook of International Trade Statistics 1977*, United Nations, New York, vol. 1, 1978, Table B, pp. 64–67.

2. Statement by Viscount Etienne Davignon, as the European Community's Commissioner for Industrial Affairs, to the European Parliament, Strasbourg, 9 May 1978. See the *Financial Times*, 11 May 1978.

3. For a discussion of the European Community's steel cartel in an historical context, see Kent Jones, 'Forgetfulness of Things Past: Europe and the Steel Cartel', *The World Economy*, May 1979. The whole issue of cartels is closely analysed in Jan Tumlir, 'Salvation Through Cartels? On the Revival of a Myth', *The World Economy*, October 1978.

4. The implications of the trigger-price mechanism of the United States were set out in Matthew J. Marks, 'Remedies to "Unfair" Trade: American Action against Steel Imports', *The World Economy*, January 1978, where the difficulties of continuing the system for long were foreshadowed.

5. *Financial Times*, 19 June 1978, p. 1.

6. *Ibid.*

7. Commission of the European Community, 'A Steel Policy for Europe', *European File*, Brussels, June 1979, p. 2.

8. This does not seem to be the case. See 'Europe's Unclubbable Steelmakers', *Financial Times*, 2 February 1979, where it is reported that the Davignon guidelines 'have been broken time and time again by member companies'.

9. *The Economist*, 8 November 1980, p. 56.

10. *Seventh Report on Competition Policy* (Brussels: Commission of the European Community, 1977) p. 181.

11. *Financial Times*, 18 July 1979, p. 17.

12. Commission of the European Community, 'A Steel Policy for Europe', *op. cit.*, p. 5.

13. *Financial Times*, 2 February 1979, p. 5.

14. *Financial Times*, 10 October 1980, p. 1.

15. *Financial Times*, 19 July 1978, p. 8.

16. *Financial Times*, 17 January 1978, p. 22.

17. *Financial Times*, 16 May 1978, p. 36.

18. *International Herald Tribune*, Paris, 16 May 1978, p. 9.

19. *Financial Times*, 4 April 1978, p. 22.

20. *Financial Times*, 1 December 1979, p. 1.

21. Statement by the Chairman of AWES, Mr Rijka, reported in the *Financial Times*, 18 March 1978, p. 21.

22. *Seventh Report on Competition Policy, op. cit.*, p. 139.

23. *Eighth Report on Competition Policy* (Brussels: Commission of the European Community, 1979) para. 182.

24. *The Economist*, 24 June 1978, pp. 89 and 90.

25. *GATT Multilateral Trade Negotiations*, Communication from the Commission to the Council of Ministers, Com. (79)514 (Brussels: Commission of the European Community, 1979) para. 4.1.

26. *Financial Times*, 9 May 1978, p. 5.

27. *The Economist*, 24 June 1978, p. 89.

28. *The Tokyo Round of Multilateral Trade Negotiations*, Report of the Director-General of the GATT (Geneva: GATT Secretariat, 1979) pp. 132–36.

29. *Financial Times*, 9 May 1978, p. 5.

30. *Financial Times*, 18 May 1978, p. 5.

31. *Ibid.*

32. *Financial Times*, 23 June 1978.

33. Courtaulds, ICI, Rhône-Poulenc, Akzo, Bayer, Hoechst, Montefibre, SNIA, Anich, SIR and Fabelta.

34. *Financial Times*, 23 June 1978.

35. The formal title for the MFA is the Arrangement Regarding International Trade in Textiles. The multilateral system of quotas on developing-country exports of textiles to developed-country markets began with the Short Term Arrangement of 1961, which was replaced by the Long Term Arrangement (LTA) of 1962, which was extended a number of times. Both arrangements were confined to cotton textiles. But in 1973 was negotiated the MFA, which came into force in 1974 and was extended in 1978 after the European Community had negotiated, under a protocol to the MFA, a series of bilateral quota agreements.

For a thorough discussion of the above arrangements, looking both back and forward, see Donald B. Keesing and Martin Wolf, *Textile Quotas against Developing Countries*, Thames Essay No. 23 (London: Trade Policy Research Centre, 1980).

36. *Eleventh General Report*, 1977 (Brussels: Commission of the European Community, 1978) para. 462.

37. *Financial Times*, 6 June 1978, p. 1.

38. *Financial Times*, 12 June 1978, p. 25.

39. *Financial Times*, 8 February 1978, p. 23.
40. *Financial Times*, 31 May 1978, p. 46.
41. *Financial Times*, 22 May 1978, p. 3.
42. See Note 35 above.
43. *Financial Times*, 22 May 1978, p. 3.
44. Jacques Attali, *Le Monde*, Paris, 27 December 1978, p. 24.

CHAPTER FIVE

Alternatives to Delayed Structural Adjustment in 'Workshop Europe'

There is much to criticise in the way in which industrial policy is conducted in the European Community. Governments continue to fly to the help of sick firms without apparently considering the broader implications of such aid for other sectors of the world economy. It is necessary to think in terms of the world economy because of the degree of integration which has taken place among national economies, especially among the more industrialised ones, as a result not only of the liberalisation of international trade and capital flows that has been effected since World War II but also of the technological advances that have been made since then in transport and communications; and it is still necessary to labour the point because, in spite of all the political talk of 'economic inter-dependence', it is not yet obvious that politicians and media of public opinion have much idea of what it means. Restructuring an industry has in practice become synonymous, in the European Community, with protection and cartelisation and there is a deep reluctance to let large firms, however inefficient, go to the wall.[1]

Even so, a definite change is discernible. Governments, perhaps for the first time since World War II, are prepared to *help* industry in its search for rationalisation. Far from preventing firms from closing marginal plants for employment reasons, they are now making aid *conditional* on plans for scrapping inefficient plant and cutting jobs (except maybe in Italy). This change in attitude has been forced on otherwise reluctant governments by Western Europe's altered position in the world economy. Western Europe is dependent on external suppliers for energy, raw materials and food. It therefore cannot stop trading and in order to trade it must be competitive. Yet, instead of being one of only two poles of industrial development in the world supplying the entire globe with manufactures, Western Europe is now entering an era where it will be one of several, perhaps five or six, centres of industry.

Full Costs of Stretching the Process of Adjustment

Although the change in attitude is discernible, the governments of the European Community and the Commission are still using policies which date from the time when Western Europe could afford to be inefficient. Thus the use by the Community of protection and cartelisation in the steel and fibre industries is fraught with dangers for other sectors of the economy. The 'breathing space' argument in favour of these policies rests on the assumption that adjustment is easier and less costly if it is spread out over a number of years. This is questionable. First, the damage to the rest of the economy is greater the longer a stricken industry is allowed to prolong the agony and, secondly, it is not obvious that prolonged adjustment is really any easier to bear than quick surgery. Even the direct costs may turn out, in practice, to be higher.

An example taken from the British steel industry will serve to make the point. The Shelton Works, belonging to the British Steel Corporation (BSC), employing some 3000 workers and making 164 000 tons of steel a year, had been losing some £12 million a year since 1975.[2] Finally in June 1978, 1500 workers were dismissed, the others were transferred elsewhere and the plant was closed – a courageous decision. The British Government had kept 1500 people employed for three and a half years at a cost of £36 million. Each job had by then cost the British taxpayer £24 000 besides producing half a million tons of unwanted steel. Would it not have been better for all concerned – BSC, the Government, the workers and the taxpayers – if in 1975 the redundant employees had been offered, say £16 000 each (two year's savings from closing the plant) and called it a day for the Shelton Steel Works? As it is, the taxpayers' money is locked up in unsaleable (unless subsidised) steel and the dismissed work force is disgruntled at the low level of severance pay. Nothing has been gained by putting off the decision for three and a half years.

What is true for BSC is true for a whole economy even if the figures are staggering. The very magnitude of the structural change being imposed on the European Community's declining industries is such that quick surgery and generous redundancy payments are likely to be deemed 'too expensive'. Yet the full costs of spreading the process of adjustment over several years would be a multiple of this. What are they?

For a start there are the indirect costs discussed in connection with the Davignon Plan for steel and which apply to almost any sector of industry:

(a) Delay in adjustment will raise prices whether directly for finished products or indirectly for intermediate products. The increase in price multiplied by the quantity consumed constitutes an uncomputed and unvoted tax of considerable magnitude on people's incomes.

(b) The increase in price will affect the industry's ability to compete abroad and at home. In the case of an intermediate product, this effect extends to other home products which use it as an input.

(c) The creation of a sheltered market and suppression of competition within it removes the only objective measure of efficiency and will result in a wasteful use of resources within the protected sector.

(d) As a result of protection, the diversion of surplus production from other countries to third markets will further undermine the export competitiveness of both protected and related industries.

(e) Protection may provoke direct retaliation or, more subtle and just as damaging, indirect trade displacement in unrelated industries which presumably enjoy a comparative advantage.

(f) Newly industrialising countries will be stimulated into climbing faster up the ladder of economic development and cause problems to emerge elsewhere: if one tries to avoid structural adjustment in one sector, it tends to re-emerge somewhere else.

As if these pitfalls were not enough, there are several more which, because they are third-order or fourth-order effects, are not often specified or even perceived. Thus subsidies to inefficient firms constitute a tax on efficient ones. This is no way to foster growth and productivity. Furthermore, the price distortions and efficiency losses mentioned above are just the beginning of several causal chains which may lead to multiple reductions in incomes. One chain runs as follows. As people's real incomes are reduced they have less to spend on other goods. This means that more efficient sectors are deprived of the growth in demand which would normally allow them to expand. As a result, the direst predictions that the market economy is incapable of providing alternative employment to people in stricken industries may be fulfilled *as a result* of the policies adopted to help them. If this causes a reinforcement of job-protection measures the causal chain becomes a vicious circle. If, on the other hand, governments attempt to maintain people's real incomes while at the same time prolonging adjustment the result will be inflation. This will, in time, reduce investment, and hence reduce jobs and incomes, and set in motion the process described previously.

Another point is that delaying adjustment will tie up productive resources in a low-productivity and low-efficiency activity, thus raising the price of resources for more efficient sectors at best, or starving them of resources at worst, thereby reducing their competitiveness. Ultimately, a prolonged misallocation of productive resources, even if the *trend* is towards rather than away from comparative advantage, may permanently handicap the newer sectors, if other countries are at the same time adapting more quickly. By the time the slowly adapting countries get there, their competitors are liable to be well down the learning curve for new industries and they may never really catch up with them in terms of efficiency and unit costs. It could be argued that this is happening to the European Community in micro-processors and their multiple applications: while people in the Community suspiciously circle this new field of technology with a mixture of disbelief and apprehension, others have eagerly picked it up. Their entrepreneurial talents have not been locked into steel or textiles.

Alternative Policies

There are basically two alternatives to the type of industrial policy at present pursued in most West European countries. The first would be not to have one at all. This is by no means as outrageous a suggestion as one might think, for one could soften the blow for individual workers losing their jobs by providing them with generous severance pay, related to the potential savings due to the closure of the inefficient plants. This would have the advantage of making most socially acceptable the elimination of the least viable sectors. In the meantime, constraints on the expansion of new sectors would be lifted; and in such circumstances it is likely that at least as many viable new jobs would develop as unviable old ones are lost.

Several examples of this process of structural adjustment can be cited: the running down of the Swiss watch industry, which occurred while an alternative micro-engineering industry was built up; the rationalisation of the West German textile industry coupled with the steady expansion of the chemical and mechanical engineering sectors; and the streamlining of Japanese steel and shipbuilding activities coinciding with the expansion of the automobile and electronic sectors.

There being only a limited amount of fungible capital and entrepreneurship in an economy at any point in time, it is self-evident that the dynamic sectors *cannot* grow *unless* the ailing ones are allowed to shrink. As for jobs, they are surely more secure and better paid in thriving than in sickly sectors. Whether, in the aggregate, supply and demand in the labour market achieve reasonable equilibrium depends far more on encouraging new sectors to thrive than on the government 'guaranteeing' full employment with 'appropriate' fiscal and monetary policies, because of the well-known inflexibility of wages in a downward direction.

The measure of a society's capacity for change would be a combination of a structural shift in employment and an ability to maintain real incomes (and if possible increase them). The American economy in the 1970s showed itself capable of this. Thus, while employment in manufacturing declined, employment in the service sector expanded so rapidly that it not only took up most of the slack from industry, but absorbed 15 million new entrants into the labour market also. Meanwhile industrial production increased and real incomes rose. Even in the United Kingdom, where jobs have been lost in steel-making, textiles and mechanical engineering, the aggregate number of people employed in manufacturing has not declined in the decade since 1970. This implies that employment has risen elsewhere.

It does seem clear, however, that the process in the United Kingdom is not a smooth and easy one. If this is accepted as a working hypothesis, then it is legitimate to ask which is the most efficient means available of easing the process of structural adjustment.

The first-best policy, in an abstract sense, would be to identify the reasons for the malfunctioning of labour and capital markets and rectify them (some reasons are suggested below). But this is a long-term programme and results are needed quickly. For this reason, it is suggested that special incentives should be offered to make change more attractive – that is, by giving generous redundancy payments to the 'victims' of change.

Part of these payments can be viewed as constituting the cost to society of making a clean break with the past; the remainder would be a straight transfer from the rest of society – a one-off payment to get people to adjust who otherwise would be a long-term burden on the others.

A second strategy, if one believes that governments have a role to play in this domain, would be to adopt policies to *accelerate* structural change. This seems to have been the policy of Japan.[3] It would involve the aggressive running down of ailing sectors and the concomitant building up of selected growth industries. There are two dangers here: first, the government is not likely to get the mixture of industries to axe and ones to encourage quite right; and secondly, replacement of the market by the government as allocator of the nation's resources raises the familiar question of the link between economic systems and individual liberty. But at least this strategy has the virtue of pursuing economic efficiency aggressively. Industrial policy in most West European countries does not do this and thus they have the worst of both worlds – a slowing down of structural change and a growing threat to their cherished liberties. This is unintelligent and short-sighted radicalism.

What constructive suggestions could one make for breaking out of this policy trap? There are several steps which would help to reduce rigidities in both labour and capital markets which would promote restructuring while making ample provision for legitimate social demands.

Labour-market Distortions

Attention will be focussed first on labour markets.[4]

1. Redundancy Payments by the State: Job-security legislation as it now stands in many West European countries has a distorting effect on the economy. First, by making it costly to dismiss workers when required, it discourages firms from engaging labour on long-term contract in the first place. Firms prefer to work with full order-books and long delivery terms, rather than expand capacity to meet demand. Temporary employment flourishes, which decreases job security for all new employees, a result which is the exact opposite of legislators' intentions. Finally, in cases where the present discounted value of the future gains from rationalisation (likely to be under-estimated) are less than the immediate cost of redundancy payments, the law discourages efficiency because it is cheaper to continue with inefficient methods of production than to dismiss redundant workers. The same social objective, compensation for loss of gainful employ-ment through no fault of one's own, could be achieved and the above-mentioned inefficiencies avoided if redundancy payments were made by the state, rather than by the firms, as suggested earlier.

This would not increase government expenditure over time because savings would be made (i) in stopping subsidies to non-viable firms and (ii) in lower unemployment insurance payments as employers would no longer be discouraged from creating new jobs.

2. Wage Flexibility and Flat-rate Taxation: A policy of minimum wages, steeply progressive personal taxes and redistribution of income distorts the labour market in the long run. It reduces the supply of skilled labour (for why should one make the effort of acquiring a skill if one's real disposable income is not appreciably higher as a result?) and, at the same time, increases the supply of unskilled labour, which is already often in excess supply at the (high) minimum wage rates. The real tragedy is that skilled and unskilled labour are complementary factors of production. One skilled person 'creates' work for several unskilled ones. The shortage of the former thus adds to the unemployment of the latter.

It is significant in this respect that there is a chronic shortage of skilled people in the United Kingdom, even in periods of high unemployment, while occasionally one observes in West Germany a shortage of unskilled labour, coupled with unemployment among the highly skilled. Both paradoxical situations can be traced, in part, to constraints on the supply of one type of labour: under-supply of skilled individuals in the United Kingdom due to the tax system and restrictive trade-union practices; and under-supply of unskilled individuals in West Germany due to restrictions on the immigration of foreign labour.

The capacity of the West European labour market to adjust smoothly to structural changes in the demand for different types of labour would be enhanced by allowing after-tax and post-allowance incomes to reflect more faithfully the economy's relative needs. This, in turn, implies greater wage flexibility and a flat-rate tax structure.

3. Regional Welfare Differentials: Attachment to the principle of the unitary wage – equal pay for equal work throughout the country – creates pockets of high unemployment in areas from which people do not wish to move and to which industries do not wish to go. Larger regional wage differentials would help to create employment in peripheral areas and would encourage mobility.

4. Improved Unemployment Insurance: Unemployment insurance already exists in all West European countries and undoubtedly already goes a long way to improving job mobility by giving people a 'breathing space' in which to adapt to a change of circumstances. It could be improved, however, in order to tailor it more closely to people's individual needs. Thus, most workers, especially the young, need steeply degressive temporary unemployment benefits to tide them over a period of job-hunting, while still encouraging them to 'hunt' seriously. Older people may wish to withdraw from the labour force altogether or seek part-time work.

In order to reduce moral hazard and maintain the incentive to look for a new job, unemployment insurance needs to be highly differentiated and put on an actuarilly sound basis. This probably implies that the state should set the framework, by establishing minimum levels of cover (as it does already in third-party automobile insurance) and letting the private insurance market do the rest. People would then be free to choose the type of unemployment insurance they think fits their particular needs best.

5. Relieving Burden on Entrepreneurial Activity: Much social legislation (such as job security, minimum wages, employer liability, worker representation) is passed on the assumption that the large, successful and prosperous firm is the norm and that laws are needed to redress the balance in favour of labour. This has the effect of discouraging small firms. The gradual demise of the small firm has undesirable consequences for the economy, especially the weakening of competition and the loss of flexibility in the face of changing tastes or technology. And this without mentioning the long-term political danger of increasing concentration, namely that large firms in concentrated industries become easy targets for nationalisation and even in private hands cannot always be relied upon to support the market system.

The answer is probably not to start differentiating between large and small firms before the law, which would be seeking to correct one distortion by creating another, but to lighten the burden placed on entrepreneurial activity *per se*. This in itself might be enough to provide the necessary competitive counterweight to large firms. In any event, the simplistic vision of the capitalist exploiting the worker is no longer credible nowadays (if indeed it ever was) as a reason for systematically discouraging the productive process. Far from diverging, the interests of labour and capital coincide; and the firms and countries where this is understood tend to be considerably more 'successful' (in terms of conventional commercial measures) than those where the mythical conflict is carefully nurtured for political reasons: take, for example, the contrast between Japan and Switzerland, on the one hand, and Britain and Italy, on the other; or between International Business Machines (IBM), which has never had a strike, and British Leyland, where striking has become the normal method of negotiation.

Capital-market Distortions

Attention will turn now to capital markets.

1. Incentives for Risk Capital: Corporate tax rates are already high at 50 per cent, but current tax legislation in most countries subjects corporate profits to double taxation, once at the company level and again at the shareholder's level. This must tend to discourage private individuals from investing in stocks and shares, obliging firms to turn increasingly to banks and institutional investors. This may be one of the reasons for industrialists' frequent complaint that modern stock markets force upon them short-term profit-maximising behaviour by assigning low values to high-risk ventures. It is axiomatic that institutions tend to avoid risky choices, because the careers of the individuals that compose them depend on 'not rocking the boat' and on 'fitting in well'. These values are difficult to combine with risk-taking entrepreneurship.

In this connection, it should also not be forgotten that investment income is often taxed at higher rates than 'earned' income and that, if the recipient is in a high marginal tax bracket, the post-tax return on an investment in shares is likely to be negligible. It is hardly surprising that under these circumstances the stock market ceases to be an efficient institution for channelling risk capital to firms which need it.

Meanwhile, very high risk capital, which seeks its reward through spectacular capital gains, simply melts away if capital gains taxes are levied at punitive rates. As a result, small firms collapse for want of funds or are absorbed by large ones looking for youth and renewal, the spirit of independent entrepreneurship is stifled and the economy becomes progressively concentrated. And where does risk capital find a refuge? Abroad – and in gold, real estate and casinos (the flight to which is also favoured by inflation).

2. Charges for Publicly-provided Goods: The excessive recourse by governments to the capital market deprives corporations of the public's non-risk savings at undistorted rates of interest. When public borrowing reaches the level of 7 to 13 per cent of GNP, as it has in some years in Britain and Italy, it is difficult to avoid the conclusion that private investment is being 'crowded out'. In the absence of massive government borrowing, interest rates would have been lower and private investment higher.

The solution is not always easy. Government deficits are partly the result of past legislation and expenditure cannot be changed radically unless one alters the law of the land – which takes time and political will. What can be done even in the short run, as the Thatcher Government in Britain has shown, is to increase charges levied by public corporations and to make marginal but still significant changes in the amount or quality of public services.

The golden rule for reform, however, if people wish to avoid being squeezed out by a steadily expanding state sector, is never to have a job done by a public body which could be done by a private one. Since this would constitute a massive reform – the hiving off of 40 per cent of the British Government's total expenditure for a start[5] – one might start with the more modest but still fairly effective step of charging for publicly-provided private goods according to cost. The need for one or other of these reforms is urgent, for without such a change governments will be increasingly forced into inflationary financing of their budget deficits, which creates yet further negative interactions. It is encouraging to note that the Thatcher Government has already gone a long way to establishing a strong link between price and cost in the public sector.

3. Impact of Inflation on Investment: Inflation distorts investment decisions by increasing uncertainty and forcing firms to opt for short-term ventures with a safe and quick pay-off.[6] With inflation rates of over 5 per cent per annum, economic uncertainty is significantly increased and perception of relative price changes is weakened, perhaps seriously. Furthermore, there is the technical problem of what value to place on assets in times of inflation, how much to allow for depreciation and how to avoid being unfairly taxed. It is not surprising that under such conditions private investment should falter.

Conclusions

The ideal industrial policy would encourage the rationalisation of industry with once-only redundancy or relocation payments financed by the state as an alternative to quasi-permanent subsidisation of loss-making firms. The budgetary cost would be high in the short run. But it would be lower in the long run than pouring good money after bad into essentially non-viable enterprises. The *laissez faire* liberal might object to so much state aid to ease the process of adjustment, but if one is prepared to leave the sphere of economics to argue the case for the market mechanism, then logically one must be prepared to take account of the political problems arising from its application.

Subsidies to firms *per se* should be stopped so as to restore the incentive for managers to perform as market-oriented entrepreneurs. At present too many of their talents are directed toward optimising their relationship with government departments, because that is where the greatest return on effort is to be found.

More generally, government could improve the flexibility of the economy by reducing some of the labour-market and capital-market distortions mentioned above, not by introducing new measures to offset market pressures, but by going to the root cause of the disfunction.

The 'intelligent radical' would go much further. He would recommend that the state be given wide powers to undertake investments in private goods which are shunned by the market, on the grounds that the government is better equipped to 'restructure' the economy than the market. In the author's opinion, the 'intelligent radical' like the sorcerer's apprentice, is almost bound to fail in the attempt because neither he nor the state can acquire the 'full knowledge which would make mastery of events possible'.[7] But this is a subsidiary problem. Even if the state could guarantee a better economic performance than the market, it would still not be wise to allow it to shape people's economic destiny for the sake of what remains of their individual liberties and pluralistic forms of government. As it is, the crisis of democracy in a country like the United Kingdom is in great measure attributable to the politisation of economic decisions; and it stands in part as a warning to the well-intentioned proponents of an extension of state powers in the name of helping structural industrial change.

As for the reliability of the idea that semi-permanent concertation between firms can produce a *better* match between supply and demand, and can prepare industry *better* for the future, than free competition, one can only point to the fact that economists (who are so notoriously divided on many issues) are unanimous in condemning cartels. Not only do cartels permit producers to cut production conveniently to fit demand, and thus avoid disagreeable price drops and/or costly over-capacity. Cartels also hinder the process of trial and error by which decentralised firms in competition with one another seek solutions to problems and sooner or later find them. It is an illusion to believe that one could replace the competitive system of trial and error by concertation because one cannot plan the innovations on the basis of which economic growth proceeds.

NOTES

1. The arguments are set out with care and rigour in Tumlir, 'Salvation Through Cartels? On the Revival of a Myth', *op. cit.*

2. *Financial Times*, 8 June 1978, p. 6.

3. See Nobuyoshi Namiki, 'Internal Adjustment Problems of Japan', in Hugh Corbet and Robert Jackson (eds), *In Search of a New World Economic Order* (London: Croom Helm, for the Trade Policy Research Centre, 1974); and also Namiki, 'Japanese Subsidy Policies', in Steven J. Warnecke (ed.), *International Trade and Adjustment Policies* (London: Macmillan, 1978) pp. 123–42.

4. For a review of labour-market problems, see Victoria Curzon Price, *Unemployment and Other Non-work Issues*, Thames Essay No. 25 (London: Trade Policy Research Centre, 1980).

5. Arthur Seldon, 'Micro-economic Controls: Disciplining the State by Pricing', *op. cit.*, pp. 75–84.

6. See Alan Greenspan, 'Investment Risk: the New Dimension of Policy', *The Economist*, 6 August 1977; and 'Trends in Industrial R & D', *OECD Observer*, Paris, March 1979.

7. F. A. von Hayek, *Full Employment at Any Price?* (London: Institute of Economic Affairs, 1975).

In this connection, British governments of either party will, over the next two decades, have to decide on how to manage North Sea oil revenues, most of which will accure to the state in the form of taxes and royalties (about £6000 million a year). This raises issues in industrial policy. How to avoid the dreaded 'Dutch disease' (that is, 'deindustrialisation')? Hot to ensure that the North Sea windfall is used to strengthen the non-oil sector of the British economy and not to weaken it? How to guarantee that Britain will make the return journey from an oil to a non-oil economy without loss of income? All this could be done by abolishing corporation tax (at present yielding £4000 million a year) which would dramatically stimulate productive investment and free the economy not only from all the distortions in allocation due to tax rebates, grants and tax holidays but also from 'the right to meddle', which the corporation tax *per se* gives the government and the civil service.

Selected Bibliography

Set out below is a selected bibliography, a very selected one, on the literature which has begun to develop on industrial policies, which in many ways is simply an extension of the subject of non-tariff barriers to trade.

ROBERT E. BALDWIN, *Non-tariff Distortions of International Trade* (Washington: Brookings Institution, 1970; and London: Allen & Unwin, 1971).
This was one of the first studies of non-tariff measures which are the instruments of what have come to be called industrial policies, although it is mostly concerned with quotas rather than the more subtle methods of non-tariff intervention.

RICHARD BLACKHURST, NICOLAS MARIAN and JAN TUMLIR, *Trade Liberalization, Protectionism and Interdependence*, GATT Studies in International Trade No. 5 (Geneva: GATT Secretariat, 1977).
The authors are at the core of the Research and Statistics Division of the GATT Secretariat and have succeeded admirably in reasserting the arguments for trade liberalisation and against protection in the context of an increasingly interdependent world.

RICHARD BLACKHURST, NICOLAS MARIAN and JAN TUMLIR, *Adjustment, Trade and Growth in Developed and Developing Countries*, GATT Studies in International Trade No. 6 (Geneva: GATT Secretariat, 1978).
This trenchant review and analysis of the impact on world trade patterns in developing countries goes on to analyse the pressures for change in developed-country economies, how 'uncertainty' affects

investment, the implementation of competition policies and labour-market developments before dealing with obstacles to adjustment. The study greatly helps to clarify complex issues that are leaving governments somewhat at a loss as to what they should be doing in a rapidly integrating world economy.

W. M. CORDEN and GERHARD FELS (eds), *Public Assistance to Industry: Protection and Subsidies in Britain and Germany* (London: Macmillan, for the Trade Policy Research Centre and the Institut für Weltwirtschaft an der Universität Kiel, 1976; and Boulder, Colorado: Westview Press, 1976).
The papers arising out of this Anglo-German study have been skilfully integrated by the editors who draw out the lessons of experience in the two countries and clarify some basic issues relating to 'public assistance', whether via protection or subsidies, to private enterprises.

GERARD and VICTORIA CURZON, *Hidden Barriers to International Trade* and *Global Assault on Non-tariff Trade Barriers*, Thames Essays Nos 1 and 3 respectively (London: Trade Policy Research Centre, 1970 and 1971 respectively).
Two early contributions to the study of non-tariff measures, instruments of industrial policy, the first being concerned with classifying the myriad ways in which governments assist the industries of their countries, the second being concerned with ways of overcoming non-tariff distortions of international competition.

GEOFFREY DENTON, SEAMUS O'CLEIREACAIN and SALLY ASH, *Trade Effects of Public Subsidies to Private Enterprise* (London: Macmillan, for the Trade Policy Research Centre, 1975; and New York: Holmes & Meier, 1975).
One of the first detailed studies of the influence of public subsidies to private enterprise in creating discriminations against imports in favour of exports at the expense of the taxpayer and the consumer.

HARRY G. JOHNSON, *Technology and Economic Interdependence* (London: Macmillan, for the Trade Policy Research Centre, 1976; and New York: St Martin's Press, 1976).
Stressing the economic character of technology, Johnson disposes of some widely-held views about economic growth, multinational

enterprises and science policy in the course of relating the development of technology to the development of the world economy.

IRVING LEVESON and JAMES W. WHEELER (eds), *Western Economies in Transition: Structural Change and Adjustment in Industrial Countries* (Boulder: Westview Press, for the Hudson Institute, 1980).
This conference volume contains a wide range of views in the papers on the problems of adjustment and how they should be addressed and reflects the conflicts that often arise between academic economists and those who have had policy-making experience.

S. C. LITTLECHILD, *The Fallacy of the Mixed Economy* (London: Institute of Economic Affairs, 1978).
In this essay are set out the arguments against those of James Meade's 'intelligent radical'.

HARALD B. MALMGREN, *International Economic Peacekeeping* (New York: Quadrangle, for the Atlantic Council of the United States, 1972).
Another early contribution to the problems of negotiating on non-tariff measures, reflecting the author's grasp of bureaucracy politics.

HARALD B. MALMGREN, *International Order for Public Subsidies*, Thames Essay No. 11 (London: Trade Policy Research Centre, 1977).
The merit of this essay is that it combines a sound analysis of the economics of public subsidies to industry with a sound grasp of the politics of coping with the problem which is at the heart of 'industrial policies' in developed countries.

JAMES E. MEADE, *The Intelligent Radical's Guide to Economic Policy: the Mixed Economy* (London: Allen & Unwin, 1975).
One of the main questions that divide contemporary economists is where the free market should end and the 'superstructure of governmental interventions and controls', to use Professor Meade's phrase, should begin. Some draw the line to afford the market as much scope as possible while others do so to afford the state as much scope as possible. In this volume the Noble Prize economist attempts to find a middle way.

ROBERT MIDDLETON, *Negotiating on Non-tariff Distortions of Trade: the EFTA Precedents* (London: Macmillan, for the Trade Policy Research Centre, 1975; and New York: St Martin's Press, 1975).
A very thorough study of EFTA's experience in dealing with non-tariff measures of relevance to broader efforts to deal with such measures.

The Tokyo Round of Multilateral Trade Negotiations, Report of the Director-General of the GATT (Geneva: GATT Secretariat, 1979). Although prepared in somewhat bland terms, this report on the results of the Tokyo Round negotiations, which included a number of codes of conduct on non-tariff measures that should serve to constrain the worst excesses of some industrial policies, will have to serve as a reference work until a more thorough report and evaluation can be prepared.

STEVEN WARNECKE (ed.), *International Trade and Adjustment Policies* (London: Macmillan, 1978).
This is something of a 'mixed bag' of essays on adjustment policies in developed countries with the two most interesting being Nobuyoshi Namiki's essay on Japanese experience and Sidney Golt's on British experience.

MARTIN WOLF, *Adjustment Policies and Problems in Developed Countries*, Working Paper No. 349 (Washington: World Bank, 1979). In this volume the author reviews the adjustment issues posed by advances in technology and import competition from developing countries in the markets of developed countries. Mr Wolf advocates 'carefully designed general industrial, regional and manpower policies' to help firms, workers and regions affected by structural decline.

Index

AEG-Telefunken, 54
agriculture, 37
aid schemes, 72–3, 75–7
Air France, 44
Andreotti, Julio, 67
Appel, Hans, 52
Association of West European Ship-
    builders (AWES), 98
Australia, 7, 86, 89

Banco di Roma, 67
banking, 54, 55, 66
bankruptcy, 47, 52, 65
Barre, Raymond, 46
Belgium, 87, 96
Benn, Anthony Wedgwood, 58
Beswick Review, 96
Boussac textile conglomerate, 106
Brazil, 86, 89
Bresciani Group, 88, 89
Bretton Woods, 1, 2
British Leyland, 53, 58–60, 62, 64,
    126
British National Oil Corporation, 63
British Steel Corporation, 61, 62, 64,
    87, 96, 97, 119
Bundesverband der Deutschen In-
    dustrie (BDA), 53
bureaucratic disfunction theory, 33

Callaghan, James, 23, 96
Canada, 3, 4, 7
capital-market imperfections, 30,
    126

Carrington Viyella, 109
cartelisation, 52, 78, 88, 104, 106,
    118
Charbonnages de France, 44
chemical industry, 99–104, 114,
    122
Chrysler, 29, 59, 60
Citroen, 45
Claes, Willy, 96
clothing industry, 104, 109–14
coal-mining, 51
Cockerill, 87, 96
Code on Subsidies and Counter-
    vailing Duties, 5, 36
Columbia, 7
Comecon countries, 89, 103
Comité   interministériel   pour
    l'Aménagement des Structures
    Industrielles (CIASI), 45, 46, 54
Committee for International Invest-
    ment and Multinational En-
    terprises, 3
compensation, 27, 28, 44
competition, 18, 20, 24, 78–9, 102
computer industry, 22, 113
Concorde, 44
Confederation General du Travail
    (CGT), 47
Conferazione   Generale   Italiano
    Lavoratori, 68
Connally, John, 67
countervailing measures, 3–5, 36
Crawley, Adrian, 49
crowding-out hypothesis, 32–3

d'Acqua, Condotte, 67
Davignon Plan, 12, 13, 88–92, 95, 120
Davignon, Viscount Etienne, 78, 88, 102, 103, 105
Decision on International Investment Incentives and Disincentives, 3
delayed structural adjustment, 118–29
Dell, Edmund, 35
Deutscher Gewerkschaftbund (DGB), 53
developing countries, 7, 17, 24, 30, 70, 93, 106
Directorate-General for Industrial Affairs, 78–9
discrimination principle, 7–9, 15
displacement effect, 76
Dunlop, 64

Eastern Europe, 24, 103, 105
economic efficiency, *see* efficiency
economic interdependence, 118
efficiency, 26–9, 35, 38
Egam, 67
employment, 122, 124
energy prices, 9
Ente Nazionale Idrocarburi (ENI), 65, 66
entrepreneurial activity, 125–6
Equity Capital for Industry Ltd, 58
Eurofer, 88, 89, 92
European Community, 3–14, 17, 21, 34, 69, 71, 103, 119, 121
  chemical industry, 99–104
  clothing industry, 104, 109–14
  competition policy, 78–9
  fibres industry, 104
  industrial policy, 72–80
  member countries' aid schemes, 72, 75
  plastics industry, 102–4
  regional policy, 73–4
  sectoral policy, 74
  shipbuilding industry, 98–9
  steel industry, 85–97
  textile industry, 104–14

trade policy, 77–8
trading relationships, 93
European Free Trade Association (EFTA), 86, 89, 108, 110
European Investment Bank, 79
European Regional Fund, 79
European Social Fund, 79
exchange of letters, 6
Export Credits Guarantee Department (ECGD), 76
exports, 6, 7, 10, 17, 78, 86, 89, 94, 107, 111

Far East, 113, 114
Feis, Herbert, 32
fibres, 102–6, 114
Finsider, 96
flat-rate taxation, 124
Fonds d'Action Conjoncturelle, 48
Fonds de Développement Economique et Social (FDES), 46
Fonds Spécial d'Adaptation Industrielle (FSAI), 48
France, 43–9, 95, 99, 104, 105, 106, 109

Galbraith, John Kenneth, 19
General Agreement on Tariffs and Trade (GATT), 1, 4–9, 21, 35, 36, 103
General Electric Co. (US), 37
Gestioni Epartci Pazioni Industriali (GEPI), 68
Giraud, André, 46
Giscard d'Estaing, President Valery, 62
government intervention, 20, 34
Greece, 113
Greenland, 74
Grierson, Ronald, 56–7
gross national product (GNP), 14, 39, 99, 127
group effect, 106
Guidelines for Multinational Enterprises, 3

Hainaut-Sambre, 96
Heath, Edward, 56

Herbert, Alfred, 58–60
Hicks, Sir John, 57
Hodgson, D. L., 21
Huller GmbH, Karl, 52

IBM, 126
ICI, 101, 108
imports, 10, 12, 14, 85, 88–9, 93–5, 111
incentives, 3–4, 17, 21, 123
income supplements, 26, 39
India, 86
indicative planning, 56, 57
Industrial and Commercial Financial Corporation, 58
Industrial Development Advisory Board (IDAB), 59
Industrial Development Certificate, 56
industrial policy, 17–83
  academic argument, 19
  aims of, 18
  alternatives, 121–8
  and market system, 25
  basic types, 18
  criticism of, 118
  definition, 17
  developing countries, 24
  European, 72–80
  France, 43–9
  Germany, 49–55
  hybrid, 23
  inherent contradiction, 33–5
  international implications, 35–7
  international regulations, 35
  Italy, 65–9
  micro-economic, 21
  negative, 18, 19
  Netherlands, 70–2
  objectives, 23
  positive, 18, 19, 33
  reasons for, 18–23
  tariff replacement by, 21
  technological change, 24
  Thatcher Government, 62–5
  United Kingdom, 55–65
industrial strategy, 33, 37
industrial structure, 17

Industry Act 1972, 56, 59, 60
Industry Act 1975, 59
inflation, 11, 23, 39, 121, 128
information-gathering system, 57
'injury' criterion, 4
Institut pour le Développement Industriel (IDI), 48
international agreements, 6–7
international economic cooperation, 1
international economic order, 1, 2, 15
International Monetary Fund (IMF), 1
International Telephones and Telecommunications (ITT), 37
International Trade Organisation (ITO), 15
international trading system, deterioration of, 9–15
investment, 31, 100, 126–8
Ireland, 74
Istituto Reconstructione Industriale (IRI), 65, 66, 96, 105
Italsider, 87, 96
Italy, 23, 65–9, 79, 87, 96, 99, 103–5, 113

Jackson, John H., 6
Japan, 7, 8, 24, 27, 84, 86, 89, 94, 98, 123, 126
job-protection measures, 23, 33, 121–4
Joseph, Sir Keith, 64

Karstadt, 52
Kindleberger, Charles, 32
Klöckner, 101
Knight, Frank H., 40
knitwear producers' agreement, 113
Küster, Georg, 50–1

labour-market imperfections, 69, 123–6
Lama, Luciano, 68
laser technology, 113
Littlechild, S. C., 21, 56

living standard, 18
loans, 79
Long Term Arrangement, 110
lump-sum compensation, 27, 28

market disruption, 5, 8
market economy, 121
market efficiency, 25
market failure, 12, 25, 29–30, 32
market fluctuations, 14, 25–6
market forces, 13, 25, 27, 33, 46, 47
market 'myopia', 32–3
market system, 26
marketing arrangements, 6
Meade, James E., 19–21, 51, 128
mechanical engineering, 122
Merseyside, 64
Merton, Robert K., 33
Michalet, Charles-Albert, 43
Michelin tyres, 3, 4
micro-processor technology, 24, 113
minimum-price system, 88, 89
Monory, René, 46
Montedison, 66, 101
Multi-fibre Arrangement (MFA), 106–7, 110
Multinational enterprises, 3, 22

National Economic Development Council, 57
National Enterprise Board, 57–63
nationalised industries, 22, 63
Neckermann, 52
Nederlandse Herstructureings-maatschappij (NEHEM), 71
Netherlands, 70–2, 104, 109
Nowzad, Bahran, 7

oil crisis, 51
oil market, 64
oil prices, 10, 11
Organisation for Economic Co-operation and Development (OECD), 3, 4, 32
Organisation of Petroleum Export-ing Countries (OPEC), 85, 86
over-capacity problem, 3, 5, 11, 12

petro-chemical industry, 84, 101

Peugeot, 45
Philips, 71
'Plan Boussac', 45
Plan de Refroidissement Fourçade, 45
planning agreements, 56
plastics industry, 102–4, 114
Portugal, 113
Price Commission, UK, 63
price control, 63
private sector, 37–9, 49, 59, 66, 67, 127
Prodi, Romano, 65
production, 11
productivity, 18, 33
protection, trade, 12, 13, 15, 25, 78, 91, 92, 98, 107, 111, 118, 120
Public Accounts Committee, 61
public borrowing, 127
public goods, 37–9
public services, 127

quotas
  import, 106–12
  production, 79, 88

recession, 22–3, 84
redundancy payments, 26, 119, 123, 124
Redundancy Payments Act 1965, 65
Regional Development grants, 56
regional policy, 73–4
regional welfare differentials, 125
Renault, 47
rescue mergers, 52
research and development, 31, 32
restructuring plan, 27, 30, 98, 118
Rhône-Poulenc, 101
risk capital, 126–7
risk-taking, 25, 26, 31, 126
Robinson, Joan, 19
robots, 11, 113
Rolls-Royce, 54, 56, 58
Rootes Motor Company, 60

Sacilor, 87
safeguards, 5–9
Schmidt, Helmut, 53

sectoral problems, 74, 84–117
security, 25, 26
Seldon, Arthur, 39
selective safeguards, 5–9
semi-conductor business, 59
sewing machines, 113
shareholders, 29, 53
Shelton Steel Works, 119
shipbuilding industry, 60, 74, 98–9, 114
Shonfield, Andrew, 50
Sindona, Michele, 67
small firms, 125, 127
Smith, Adam, 56
Societa Generale Immobiliare (SGI), 67
Societa Industria Alimentari, Milan (SIDALM), 67
Societa Italiana Resine (SIR), 67–8
South Africa, 86, 89
South Korea, 7, 24, 86, 89, 93
Spain, 89, 113
Spethmann, Dieter, 90
Stability and Growth Act, 50
stagnation, 23, 100
state aid, 29, 59–61, 64, 72, 75, 99, 118
state's function in society, 37–40
steel industry, 34, 48, 60, 74, 85–97, 115, 119, 122
steel prices, 12, 90–2
stock market, 28
structural adjustment, 20–1, 23–7, 84, 118–29
structural disease, 84–5
subsidies, 3–5, 21, 28–31, 35, 36, 41, 51, 79, 85, 86, 98, 99, 128
Switzerland, 23, 126
Systeme des Traites, 1, 2

Taiwan, 7
Talbot, 60
tariffs, 5, 17, 21, 22, 25, 27, 35, 36, 49, 77, 95, 102, 124, 126–7
technological change, 24, 85, 114
temporary employment subsidy (TES), 76
textile industry, 34, 47, 75, 76, 104–14, 122
Thatcher, Margaret, 62–5, 97, 127
Thy-Marcinelle-et-Monceau, 96
Thyssen Industrie AG, 52, 90
Tokyo Round, 2, 4, 5, 7, 9, 36, 102
trade displacement, 93
trade liberalisation, 27, 37, 78
trade policy, 37, 77, 79
trade restrictions, 6, 37, 94
trade unions, 62
'transparency' of aid systems, 72–3
Treaty of Rome, 72, 105
trigger-price mechanism, 88, 89, 95

unemployment, 11–12, 14, 124, 125
unemployment insurance, 26, 125
Unidal, 66–7
United Kingdom, 55–65, 99, 122, 124, 129
United States, 3, 4, 7, 17, 29, 32, 36, 122
Usinor, 87, 88

Volkswagen, 52, 53, 55

wage control, 63
wage flexibility, 124
West Germany, 23, 49–55, 87, 95, 97, 104, 105, 109, 124
Wilson, Harold, 56